SIGHTS AND SOUNDS OF HEAVEN

SIGHTS AND SOUNDS OF HEAVEN

THE PEARLY WHITE CITY

RONNIE S. KENNETT

XULON PRESS

Xulon Press
2301 Lucien Way #415
Maitland, FL 32751
407.339.4217
www.xulonpress.com

© 2020 by Ronnie S. Kennett

All rights reserved solely by the author. The author guarantees all contents are original and do not infringe upon the legal rights of any other person or work. No part of this book may be reproduced in any form without the permission of the author. The views expressed in this book are not necessarily those of the publisher.

Unless otherwise indicated, Scripture quotations taken from the King James Version (KJV) – *public domain*.

Printed in the United States of America.

ISBN-13: 978-1-6312-9215-6

Table of Contents

Prelude xi
Acknowledgments xv
Foreword xvii
Preface xix
Introduction xxiii

SECTION I:
IN THE BEGINNING   1

CHAPTER I: God Elohim's Plan, Purpose, and Design
  For Mankind 3
  Graphic 1B
  Graphic 2

CHAPTER II: Heaven: God's Abode, Man's Destiny 13
  Graphic 3
  Graphic 4
  Graphic 5
  Graphic 6
  Graphic 7

CHAPTER III: Names of The City of God 21
  Graphic 8
  Graphic 9
  Graphic 10
  Graphic 11
  Graphic 12

CHAPTER IV: Newness: Names, Songs, Bodies 39
**Graphic 13*
*ial*Graphic 14*
Graphic 15
Graphic 16

SECTION II:
EARTHLY COMPARISONS WITH NEW JERUSALEM   47

CHAPTER V: Comparing The Earthly Jerusalem With The New Jerusalem. 49

CHAPTER VI: New Jerusalem's Size .53
Graphic 17
Graphic 18
Graphic 19
Graphic 20

CHAPTER VII: San Antonio River Walk, Million Dollar Highway, and Magnificent Mile 61
Graphic 21
Graphic 22
Graphic 23

SECTION III:
EARTHLY AND HEAVENLY PROPHETIC EVENTS   73

CHAPTER VIII: The Rapture: "Come Up Hither" 75
Graphic 24
Graphic 25

CHAPTER IX: The Marriage Supper of The Lamb 79

CHAPTER X: The Seven-Year Great Tribulation 81

CHAPTER XI: The Second Coming of Jesus Christ and The
Battle of Armageddon...............................85
Graphic 26

CHAPTER XII: The Millennial Kingdom of Jesus Christ....87

CHAPTER XIII: The Great White Throne Judgment 91

SECTION IV:
THE PEARLY WHITE CITY 95

CHAPTER XIV: The Wall, Its Foundations, and Its
Gates of Pearl 97
Graphic 27
Graphic 28
Graphic 29
Graphic 30
Graphic 31

CHAPTER XV: The Twelve Precious Gemstones......... 109
Graphic 32

CHAPTER XVI: High Priest Breastplate/Precious Gemstones
(Old Testament) Compared To New Jerusalem's Precious
Gemstones......................................119
Graphic 33

CHAPTER XVII: The Precious Gemstone Jasper 123
Graphic 34
Graphic 35
Graphic 36
Graphic 37

CHAPTER XVIII: The Sounds of Heavenly Music........131
Graphic 38

SECTION V:
ETERNITY WITH GOD AND THE LAMB   139

CHAPTER XIX: Sights and Sounds of The Tree of Life....141

CHAPTER XX: Sights and Sounds of The River of Life....147

CHAPTER XXI: NO MORE CURSE 151
Graphic 39

CHAPTER XXII: No More Night and Super Sunday 159

CHAPTER XXIII: Reigning Forever With God The Father, Jesus Christ The Son, and The Holy Spirit.............165
Graphic 40

Special Note Of Thanks 182
Endnotes 184

PRELUDE

John 3:16
For God so loved the world, that he gave his only begotten Son,
that whosoever believeth in him should not perish,
but have everlasting life.

1 John 4:8–9
He that loveth not knoweth not God: for God is love. In this
was manifested the love of God toward us, because that God
sent his only begotten Son into the world, that we might live
through him.

"THE LOVE OF GOD"[1]

Verse I
The love of God is greater far
Than tongue or pen can ever tell;
It goes beyond the highest star,
And reaches to the lowest hell;
The guilty pair, bowed down with care,
God gave His Son to win;
His erring child He reconciled,
And pardoned from his sin.

Refrain
O love of God, how rich and pure!
How measureless and strong!
It shall forevermore endure
The saints' and angels' song.

continued

> Verse II
> When hoary time shall pass away,
> And earthly thrones and kingdoms fall,
> When men, who here refuse to pray,
> On rocks and hills and mountains call,
> God's love so sure, shall still endure,
> All measureless and strong;
> Redeeming grace to Adam's race—
> The saints' and angels' song.
>
> Verse III
> Could we with ink the ocean fill,
> And were the skies of parchment made,
> Were every stalk on earth a quill,
> And every man a scribe by trade,
> To write the love of God above,
> Would drain the ocean dry.
> Nor could the scroll contain the whole,
> Though stretched from sky to sky.
>
> Words and music written in 1917 by F. M. Lehman
> (Public domain)

We are told that the third verse of this song was written by a man with dementia who was housed in an asylum. After the man died, the profound lines of this stanza were found written on the wall of the narrow room where he had lived.[2]

God, who is *love*, created heaven and earth and made man in His image and after His likeness for His good pleasure. Also, as the omnipotent, omniscient, and omnipresent triune God, He has so much love for mankind that He included a plan, purpose, and design: He sent His Son, Jesus Christ, to die on Calvary to pay the price for our sins and provide a dwelling place for all who will receive Jesus as Savior and Lord. That dwelling place contains a new heaven, a new earth, and the new Jerusalem. His great love, grace, and mercy have extended from the third heaven to His creation of the present heaven and earth, including the garden of Eden, and will continue forever in eternity.

Acknowledgments

I dedicate this book to my darling wife, Rachel, whom I love dearly and who has faithfully been by my side for more than sixty years. She has encouraged, assisted, and inspired me with *Sights and Sounds of Heaven* presentations since their beginnings in 1991. To our daughter, Sharon, her husband, Carey; our grandson Shawn and his wife, Bethany, and their daughter and our great-granddaughter, London Olivia; daughter Rhonda, her husband, Kevin, and our grandson Andrew, and his sons and our great-grandsons, Gabriel and Austin; all of whom I thank for their love, support, and encouragement, and for truly making Rachel and me so blessed and thankful for all of you, for the love and the joy you bring to us.

To Sharon, thanks for preparing my first transparencies, revising my outlines and notes, and assisting me with this book. To Carey, Otis Bishop, and grandson Andrew, thanks for all of your help with slides and assistance with PowerPoint presentations. To my brother Mike, "Mickey," and his wife, Vickie, thanks for rearranging schedules many times to travel with Rachel and me and providing "special" heavenly music. Special thanks to my nephew, artist Jackson B. "Jack" Kennett, who painted and provided me with paintings of "The Rainbow and Noah's Ark" that are included herein. To the Rev. Bernard "Mac" McBride and Clyde R. ("C.R.") Conner, D. Phil., for their reviews and critiques of the draft of this book.

I am grateful to pastor Danny Scott and the Church of God in Bluefield, West Virginia, where I first presented "Sights and Sounds of Heaven," and to our former pastor Pat Wheeler, his wife, Jean, and the New Vision Pentecostal Holiness Church family, where Rachel and I were members for many years. To all the countless family, friends, and church family who are so very dear to me and Rachel and our family, your friendship, support, and prayers are treasured. To my brother, SMSGT Jackson "Jack" Kennett (who is now in heaven), and his wife Juanita, for their steadfast encouragement and support. Finally, to my brother, Rev. Gene Kennett, and his wife, Shirley (who is now in heaven), who unceasingly encouraged me to put "Sights and Sounds of Heaven" into a book format.

I'm sure God has a special reward for all of you, for your faithfulness to Him, and for the love, encouragement, and assistance you have given Rachel and me through the years.

Foreword

Some of the most intriguing end-of-life questions are: "What is heaven going to be like?" or "What kind of sounds will we hear?" or "Are we going to hear angels sing?" and possibly a dozen other similar questions. Since none of us have ever been there, we have little reference other than the Bible to compare or even humanly try to understand. Ron Kennett has taken this subject and, in the most wonderful way, made it simple, understandable, and viable. This book is not only easy to read but educational, humorous, worshipful, musical, inspirational, and devotional.

The two books of the Bible most often attacked for authenticity are Genesis and Revelation. It is thought that if these two can be proved incorrect, then everything between them can be considered suspect. Ron has effectively taken the Biblical truth in these books and given them spiritual veracity in a way that can be used in a classroom setting to establish theological soundness.

I found this theology on Scripture to be sound and Biblical. Even when he gives his personal feelings, there are Biblical bases that leave little for discussion. Music has been and still is a large part of Ron Kennett's life, and has definitely played a large part in forming his own personal theology. He has included many of these in the book. Many readers will recognize them and be able to relate to the words of the songs implanted and the importance music plays in faith and theology of every believer. I know you are going to enjoy this book and in addition get a glimpse of the "Sights" of heaven and even hear the "Sounds" of the music.

Clyde R. (C. R.) Conner, D. Phil.

PREFACE

In 1991, my family doctor, Dr. Norman Vaughan, was concerned that I could have prostate cancer. For a week or so, I was confined to bed rest because of a severely enlarged prostate with large nodules and an infection in my bloodstream. Dr. Vaughan referred me to a urologist, Dr. Assaad Mounzer, at Bluefield Regional Medical Center in Bluefield, West Virginia, for more tests, after which biopsies were to be performed. During that time, I began reading and studying God's Word regarding heaven, specifically the new Jerusalem.

I had accepted Jesus Christ and was saved at age fourteen and knew that God has promised His bride everlasting life and a home in heaven. Yet I had not experienced the revelation of heaven that the Holy Spirit began unfolding to me during those days. I've often shared how concerned I became, even to the point of wondering if the Lord was going to take me home to heaven.

I recall that Friday afternoon when my wife, Rachel, had gone to the pharmacy to get prescriptions refilled for me, and the telephone rang. The caller was Ferrell Hardison, a pastor from North Carolina who had preached at our West Virginia camp meeting services in Glenwood Park, during which I was privileged to lead the congregational singing.

As I recall, Ferrell had been in prayer, and the Holy Spirit began impressing him to call me. Becoming more concerned about me,

Ferrell called my office and was informed that I was at home, sick. He proceeded to call me to see what was wrong and to pray for me. Isn't that just like the Lord? I know God used Ferrell, who was hundreds of miles away, to pray the prayer of faith for me and with me! I have shared many times my firm assurance of God's healing power that day because Pastor Ferrell obeyed God on my behalf.

I am happy to tell you that the biopsies and other tests were negative…no cancer. I personally believe God healed me during this time and used this experience to give me the following (which has expanded over time) and that I have chosen to title *Sights and Sounds of Heaven.*

Interspersed throughout the chapters of this book are some pictures and slides I have used in my PowerPoint presentations over the years. My purpose in including these slides is to offer this resource material to all who may desire to use it in teaching, sermons, or other ministry presentations.

God has truly blessed Rachel and me to share *Sights and Sounds of Heaven* in many venues. He has opened the doors through which we have seen lives transformed, and we cannot express our gratitude enough to all with whom we have been privileged to share this teaching.

May I add that these opportunities arose only because of the many gracious invitations we received from pastors and churches to present "Sights and Sounds of Heaven." Thank you so very much!!

We look forward to joining you as part of the "great cloud of witnesses" (Hebrews 12:1) as we worship, adore, and serve God and the Lamb forever in heaven. Only God knows all that is prepared for His children, and I am confident we will continually be amazed in His eternal presence, forever.

May I pause here, before presenting my heartbeat about heaven and the new Jerusalem, to tell you that God and the Lamb, Jesus Christ, alone deserve all glory, honor, and praise for the content of this book.

Introduction

"Let not your heart be troubled: ye believe in God, believe also in me. In my Father's house are many mansions: if it were not so I would have told you. I go to prepare a place for you. And if I go and prepare a place for you, I will come again, and receive you unto myself; that where I am, there ye may be also." (John 14:1–3)

Jesus spoke these words to upbraid His disciples during the Passover meal, shortly before He was crucified. Jesus died on the cross for our sin(s). He was buried in a borrowed tomb and arose from the dead on the third day.

The setting for this book is "My Father's House," the new Jerusalem and the new heaven and new earth, wherein dwelleth righteousness. Finite words cannot begin to describe the glory, splendor, and beauty of all God has prepared for His family in eternity. However, as Jesus instructed John, "We are to tell those things we have seen and heard" (Revelation 22:8; Acts 4:20; Acts 22:15; 1 John 1:3). My goal is to do exactly that through the pages of this book and only by the inspiration and guidance of the Holy Spirit.

We live in uncertain times and in a chaotic, decaying, and uncertain world. But, if we know Jesus Christ as Savior and Lord, we have a "[h]ouse, not made with human hands, eternal in the heavens" (2 Corinthians 5:1). The words of the following Gospel song ring loudly and clearly to me in these perilous times:

RONNIE S. KENNETT

"The Heavenly Way"[3]

Verse I
Here on this earth with its toils and its snares,
Here where we find so much sin and despair.
There is a way filled with truth and with grace,
It was bought by the Savior who died in our place.

Refrain
There is a way to that home up above,
A way filled with glory and sweet heavenly love.
A way that is free from all sin and despair,
And it leads to those mansions in heaven so fair.

Verse II
Sometimes we wonder why heartaches and pain
Seem to drive away the sunshine and bring on the rain.
But please do not wonder or worry, dear friend,
For we have a Savior who'll go through the end.

Verse III
Jesus, He tells us, "Child, I am the way,"
I'm the way that will take you to heaven if you pray.
So let's trust in Him every hour, every day,
Unspotted and cleansed by the heavenly way.

Words and music by Ronnie S. Kennett

Today, many people are being led astray by false teachers who teach and portray different paths to heaven. These false teachers contend that all *worldly religions,* such as islam, buddhism, hinduism, new age, and many others, will lead one to heaven. They proclaim that Jesus Christ is only one of many historical prophetic figures and that Christianity is only one of many religions. How often do we hear that all religious faiths will eventually lead you to eternal life? Sadly, they are so wrong, and thus, many people are being deceived. Jesus called these teachings "the blind leading the blind" (Luke 6:39), and the apostle Peter warned that in the last days, false teachers would arise, teaching damnable heresies and deceiving many (2 Peter 2:1).

Dear friend, Jesus Christ is the only way whereby we may receive salvation and eternal life in heaven. He said in John 14:6, "I am the way, the truth, and the life: no man cometh unto the Father, but by me."

Jesus has clearly shown us in His Word that there are only two roads through this earthly life. The straight and narrow way leads to eternal life with Christ in heaven, but the broad way leads to destruction and eternal separation from God, in a burning lake of fire, which is the second death (Matthew 7:13–14; Revelation 21:8). My prayer is that any person reading this book who hasn't accepted Jesus Christ as Savior and Lord will do so and that you who are "in Christ" will rest assured, more than ever, that Jesus will soon return to rapture His bride (the church). He will take us unto Himself so that where He is, we may be also. That place, for eternity, is heaven!

Let me encourage and exhort you to use the ever-changing methods of communication to disseminate the never-changing gospel message of Jesus Christ to everyone living in your world and beyond while it is still day. Why? Because "the night cometh, when no man can work" (John 9:4), and only those whose names are written in the Lamb's book of life will live with Christ forever. As you read *Sights and Sounds of Heaven*, may you grasp more vividly a glimpse of all that awaits us, and may you share it with others.

> **HEAVEN: A GUIDE FOR TRAVELERS**
>
> - ACCOMMODATION: First Class Mansion
> - PASSPORTS: Proper Credentials
> - DEPARTURE TIMES:….Any Moment
> - TICKETS: … Written In Red …Salvation
> - CUSTOMS:…One Declaration Only-E L
> - IMMIGRATION:…Immigrants Only-U Q
> - LUGGAGE: …None Allowed or Needed
> - AIR PASSAGE: Air Travel, Short Trip

4

SECTION I

IN THE BEGINNING

Chapter I

GOD ELOHIM'S PLAN, PURPOSE, AND DESIGN FOR MANKIND

SIGHTS AND SOUNDS OF HEAVEN

THE PEARLY WHITE CITY

The Beginning: Heaven and Earth

>If ye then be risen with Christ, seek those things which are above where Christ sitteth on the right hand of God. Set your affections on things above, not on things on the earth. For ye are dead, and your

> life is hid with Christ, in God. When Christ, who is our life, shall appear, then shall we also appear with him in glory. (Colossians 3:1–4)

It has often been said, "Some people are too heavenly minded to be of any earthly good." Perhaps a more accurate saying is, "Too many of us have our heads in the clouds." The apostle Paul clearly tells us we cannot be of any earthly good unless and until we become heavenly minded. To put on the mind of Jesus Christ is to set our affections on things above, on heaven— where Christ intercedes for us at the right hand of God the Father. We cannot see, spiritually, what God desires us to do on this earth if we don't focus on things that are eternal and beyond the clouds— Heavenly things.

"Eye hath not seen, nor ear heard, neither have entered into the heart of man, the things which God hath prepared for them that love him" (1 Corinthians 2:9). I'm fully and humbly aware of this verse from the Bible and know that we cannot adequately explain the glory, beauty, and splendor of heaven. However, I am confident that the Holy Spirit reveals these things to us as we trust Him and search the Scriptures (see Colossians 2:10). That alone has sustained me and convinced me to feebly try to convey and describe the things God has planted in my heart about heaven and the new Jerusalem.

The first ten words of the Bible tell us, "In the beginning God created the heaven and the earth" (Genesis 1:1).

The apostle John's first ten words in Revelation 21:1 are, "And I saw a new heaven and a new earth."

God, Elohim (Father, Son, and Holy Spirit), created the heaven and the earth. The Triune God, through His spoken Word, said, "Let there be light" (Genesis 1:3), and in six days He created everything in and on the earth. John 1:1–3 says, "In the beginning was the Word, and the Word was with God, and the Word was God. The same was in the beginning with God. All things were made by him [Jesus]; and without him was not any thing made that was made." Hebrews 1:2 states, "his (God's) Son, whom he hath appointed heir of all things, by whom also he (Jesus) made the worlds."

Can you imagine how exciting it must have been as the Father, Son, and Holy Spirit divided the light from the darkness, made the firmament, separated the waters, made the dry land to appear with grass, herb-yielding seed, and fruit trees? Afterward, God hung two great lights in the firmament of the heaven; the sun to rule the day and the moon to rule the night. Next, the seas brought forth an abundance of sea creatures, from great whales to small fishes and even tadpoles (humor). The fowls of the air were created and began flying in earth's atmosphere, and the earth brought forth living creatures, such as cattle, beasts, and creeping things, including snakes. Just think of how our Creator must have felt as the earth came to life with all He had made.

Man: Adam, Eve, Eden

And then, on day six, God created His masterpiece...Man. Genesis 1:27 says, "male and female created he them." Man (Adam), was formed first from the dust of the ground, and after God saw it was not good for man to be alone, He caused a deep sleep to fall on Adam and made woman (Eve) from a rib in Adam's side. Beginning with day one through day five God said everything He had made was good. But, on the sixth day, after God made man and woman, He saw "it was very good" (Genesis 1:31).

God placed Adam and Eve in the garden called Eden, a beautiful paradise in which God had set in its midst the tree of life and the tree of the knowledge of good and evil. Have you given much thought to the fact that God came down and communed with Adam on a regular basis? God even brought the cattle, fowls, beasts, every living creature for Adam to name them (See Genesis 2:19). Yes, Adam and Eve knew God's voice; yet, look what happened. Of course, we know the story of man's fall and great sin after God had told Adam and Eve they could partake of every tree in Eden except the tree of the knowledge of good and evil. God had already told them, "in the day that thou eatest thereof thou shalt surely die" (Genesis 2:17). It appears to me they could possibly have eaten of the tree of life and not committed sin in doing so. What do you think?

After the serpent's deception of Eve, and after she and her husband, Adam, had eaten of the tree of the knowledge of good and evil, Genesis 3:22–24 tells us God had to drive Adam and Eve out of the garden of Eden "lest he [Adam] put forth his hand, and take also of the tree of life, and eat, and live forever." What a tragedy for Adam and Eve and for the human race. Man was driven out of this beautiful paradise because of sin and disobedience. God placed at the entrance of the garden cherubim and a flaming sword, which turned every way to *keep* the way of the tree of life. I am confident that this tree of life will be the same tree of life species in the new Jerusalem and that we will partake of it while enjoying its delicious fruit. Please take note of the word *keep*, which is used in the King James Version (KJV). We will explore this subject later (chapter XIX).

6,000 Years: From the Earth to the Moon

When writing about God's creation of the heaven and the earth, of America's astronauts and various space shuttle trips into outer space and especially to the moon, I recall the Apollo 11 spaceship named Columbia left earth on July 16, 1969, headed to the moon with astronauts Neil Armstrong, Buzz Aldrin, and Michael Collins. On July 20, 1969, Armstrong and Aldrin entered the Eagle and headed for the lunar surface, touching down on the moon's Sea of Tranquility. Upon landing, Armstrong became the first astronaut to step and walk on the moon's surface as he uttered the famous words: "That's one small step for man, one giant leap for mankind." They placed a plaque on the moon's surface that stated: "HERE MEN FROM THE PLANET EARTH SET FOOT UPON THE MOON, JULY 1969, A.D. WE CAME IN PEACE FOR ALL MANKIND."[5]

In 1972, during the Apollo 17 space trip to the moon, Gene Cernan became the last man to walk on the moon (to date). Cernan spoke to his audience from the moon and made the following quotes: "Cernan stated that standing on the surface of the moon he felt like he was looking at the Earth from 'God's front porch.'" He also made the following powerful comments: "The earth doesn't tumble through space; it moves with logic and certainty and with beauty beyond comprehension,…It's just too beautiful to have happened by accident. There has to be somebody bigger than you and me that put it all together. There is no question in my mind that there's a Creator of the universe. There's a God up there."[6]

May I add to Eugene Cernan's quotes from the moon that he was right: our Creator did create the present heaven and the earth, and sometime in the future, (perhaps soon) after the millennial reign (that is, the thousand-year reign described in Revelation 20) and white throne judgment, He will create the new heavens and a new earth wherein dwelleth righteousness (Isaiah 65:17 and 2 Peter 3:13).

While writing the above I am reminded of a gospel song written by a dear friend, Bill Franklin who lived in Roanoke, Virginia, and is now in heaven. Sputnik, the first satellite, had been launched on October 4, 1957, by Russia and Bill was on his way from church that night when he saw the heavenly happenings. Bill wrote the following song (and another song contained in this book). His daughter, Eula Franklin Sears, who has the authority to let me include these songs herein, has graciously given me written permission to do so:

"THE PEARLY MOON'S NO STOPPING PLACE FOR ME"[7]

Verse I

I've been watching for the coming back of Jesus Christ the king,
I've been looking up toward heaven, singing glory to His name.
But I'm living in a busy world, space travel's all in bloom,
How long I hear them shout and say, before we reach the moon.

Refrain

That pretty moon God put up there's no stopping place for me,
My ticket reads for a trip above, to a glory jubilee.
I've fought the fight, I've kept the faith, my homeland I can see,
And I know that pretty moon up there's, no stopping place for me.

Verse II

That yellow moon has paved the way, since days of long ago,
It smiled the night I walked to church after God had
saved my soul.
Now a brighter light guides me tonight, to the shores of
heavens blue,
Through this earthly veil on above I'll sail waving goodbye
to the moon.

Verse III
The rockets zoom on out in space, and the satellites they fly,
But no powers ever can erase God's wonders in the skies
And the glories God's built up above where the saints shout glad and free.
Again I say that pretty moon's no stopping place to me.

Words and Music by Bill Franklin

NOAH, THE ARK, CLOUDS, RAIN, GOD'S JUDGMENT, RAINBOW, AND COVENANT

While Adam and Eve failed to listen to God's voice, even though God (Elohim) made them in His image and after His likeness, remember, God gave Adam specific instructions and even came down and talked with him in the cool of the day. Yet, Adam and Eve didn't listen, did they? I'm confident that God didn't want to drive Adam and Eve out of the garden of Eden, but He did so. Why? Because, God is Holy and would not allow sin then, just as He doesn't today.

Later, Cain murders his brother, Abel, after which Seth is born (see Genesis chapter 4). Adam's genealogy is set forth in chapter 5, which includes Enoch, who walked with God and was translated that he would not see death, and his son, Methuselah, who died when he was nine hundred sixty-nine years of age, and is known as the oldest man who ever lived. Genesis chapter 6 clearly tells us how wicked, corrupt, and violent men had become (verses 5–13). That is why God instructed Noah to build an ark for the salvation of Noah and his family as well as housing two or seven of all living creatures, including animals, fowls of the earth and the air. Until this time there had never been clouds in the skies or rain on the earth. Noah listened and obeyed God, and after one hundred years, at age six hundred, Noah, his family, and every animal, fowl, and other living creatures of the flesh entered the ark—after which God shut the door to the ark, and the rains descended upon the earth. Sadly, every human being and every other living creature on the earth died in the flood that covered the whole earth. I should point out that calculations of Methuselah's life indicate that he died the same year God sent the flood.

The Bible, the variety of colors throughout the earth, and the rainbow all present evidence that God loves color. We know a rainbow is composed of the entire spectrum of colors of visible light, from the longest wavelength, red, to the shortest wavelength, violet. The order of the seven colors in a rainbow is easily remembered by the mnemonic formula ROY G. BIV: R=red, O=orange, Y= yellow, G=green, B=blue, I=indigo and V=violet. Red is at the top edge of the rainbow, and violet is at the bottom edge with the other colors in between.[8] Let me add that God set the rainbow in the sky to tell Noah (and us) that He will never destroy the earth again by a flood of water. He orchestrated the specific color spectrum with a specific number of colors that never change, and He called the rainbow "My Bow" (Genesis 9:12–17). I recall hearing Rev. Morris Cerullo state that God has a perfect plan, purpose, design, and destiny for His children.[9] I certainly believe Morris is right, and God's bow proves it.

SIGHTS AND SOUNDS OF HEAVEN

CHAPTER II

HEAVEN: GOD'S ABODE, MAN'S DESTINY

> **HEAVEN**
>
> - ETERNITY….with God..Our Father..Jesus Christ..Our Savior and Lord….The Holy Spirit….Our comforter and guide
> - NEW JERUSALEM….City of gold…Wall of JASPER..12 Gates of pearl…River of Life…Street of gold…Tree of life…12 Foundations..

Eternity with God

I have heard many ministers refer to Jesus using the following quote: "I didn't say this (life) would be easy…I only said it would be worth it (eternal life)," and I probably have made that quote, too. Of course, I don't find this quote by Jesus in the Bible.

However, contrary to many beliefs, Jesus never promised His children flowery beds of roses in this life. He did tell us in Matthew 11:28–30, "Come unto me, all ye that labour and are heavy laden, and I will give you rest...For my yoke is easy, and my burden is light." Yoke refers to a pair of balances or scales to be used in labor and work.[11] For we must work in His vineyard while it is day, for the night cometh, when no man can work (John 9:4). Although He has promised to always be with us (Matthew 28:20, "lo, I am with you alway, even until the end of the world"), to lighten the load and to ease the laborious burdens that may come our way, His Word did not say this life would be easy; however, I believe He assures us "heaven will be worth it all."

I never said it would be easy... I only said it would be worth it.

[12]

We may suffer trials and tribulations in this life, but Our Lord will deliver us out of them all, and heaven will surely be worth it all. You see, heaven is more than just a lovely word and more than a seemingly faraway land. Heaven is more than beautiful pictures painted by human hands. Heaven is God's abode and man's destiny—but *only* through the sacrificial death and shed blood of God's only begotten Son, our Savior and Lord, Jesus Christ. Heaven is *eternity* with God, our Father; Jesus Christ, our Savior; and the Holy Spirit, our comforter and guide.

Many people have asked me to define eternity. My answer is: eternity is *God*! He alone is triune, everlasting, and eternal, and He has created and made all things. Just think… soon we will live in eternity…I am including the following song lyrics that I wrote in 1978 that express how important it is for us to be ready to meet our Lord:

"THE CIRCLE OF GOD'S LOVE"[13]

Verse I
This old world is filled with hatred, sin and strife,
People seek for pleasure, not a Christ-like life.
They seem not to realize that one day soon
Jesus will return at morning, night or soon.

Refrain
But are we living in the circle of God's love?
Do we feast on hidden manna from above?
Are we walking with the Lord,
Trusting in His holy word?
Are we living in the circle of God's love?

Verse II
War and strife will flee away when Christ returns,
Within the Christian's heart this longing surely burns.
What a glorious time my friend, that's going to be,
When our Savior shall return for you and me.

continued

> *Refrain (with Tag)*
> *But, are we living in the circle of God's love?*
> *Do we feast on hidden manna from above?*
> *(Tag) When we rise to meet Christ there, at that meeting in the air.*
> *Will we be living in the circle of God's love?*
> *(Tag) Glorified with Christ I'll be throughout all eternity,*
> *If I am living in the circle of God's love.*

> Words and music by Ronnie S. Kennett

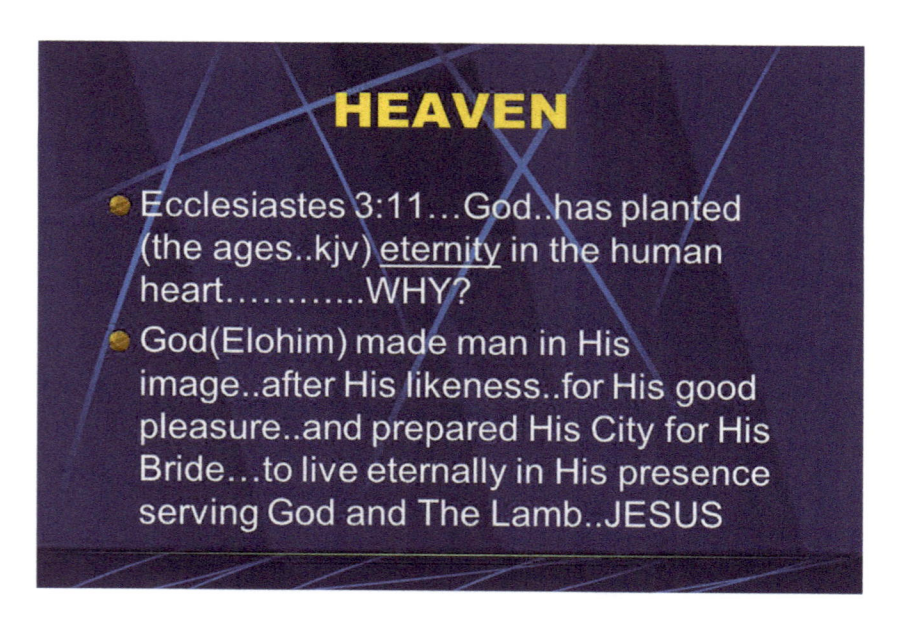

HEAVEN

- Ecclesiastes 3:11...God..has planted (the ages..kjv) eternity in the human heart............WHY?
- God(Elohim) made man in His image..after His likeness..for His good pleasure..and prepared His City for His Bride...to live eternally in His presence serving God and The Lamb..JESUS

Ecclesiastes 3:11 states: "He [God] hath...set the world [eternity, the ages] in their heart [the heart of every human being]." Why? I believe God has placed a hunger in every human heart that can only be satisfied by yielding to Him, accepting His love, worshipping Him, and serving Him. This can only happen when we receive Jesus Christ as Savior and Lord. There is no other way! Men (all-inclusive) are feverishly seeking satisfaction from the lusts of the flesh and other worldly things. The lust of the flesh, the lust of the eye, and the pride of life, which John warned us about in 1 John 2:16, are destroying many young and old alike today because they search for earthly things to satisfy their hungry fleshly appetites. This hunger will never be satisfied unless and until they turn to God through Jesus Christ.

Simply put, earthly things cannot and will not satisfy the eternal yearning of man's human heart or spiritual heart! Atheists, agnostics, Satan worshippers, and any who search for satisfaction through false religions or other worldly means will recognize this truth one day. The apostle Paul penned the Holy Spirit's words well: "Wherefore God also hath highly exalted him, and given him a name which is above every name: That at the name of Jesus every knee should bow, of things in heaven, and things in earth, and things under the earth; And that every tongue should confess that Jesus Christ is Lord, to the glory of God the Father" (Philippians 2:9–11).

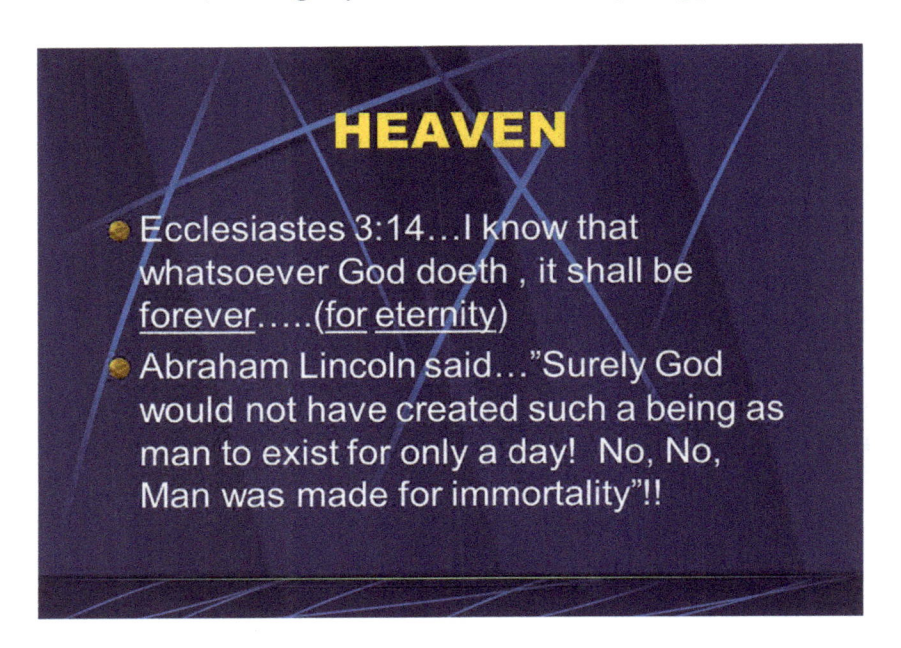

HEAVEN

- Ecclesiastes 3:14…I know that whatsoever God doeth, it shall be forever…..(for eternity)
- Abraham Lincoln said…"Surely God would not have created such a being as man to exist for only a day! No, No, Man was made for immortality"!!

Ecclesiastes 3:14 says, "whatsoever God doeth, it shall be for ever [for eternity]." President Abraham Lincoln is quoted as saying, "Surely God would not have created such a being as man, with an ability to grasp the infinite, to exist only for a day! No, no, man was made for immortality."[14] I wholeheartedly agree with President Lincoln. We will all live forever somewhere. The question is will it be heaven or hell? God made us free moral agents with a choice. I have chosen heaven: how about you? If you aren't saved, accept Jesus Christ as Savior and Lord right now. Please don't wait another moment! I promise you, reading the remainder of this book will be a glorious experience.

Our finite minds cannot grasp the depth of God's love, nor can we absorb the full meaning of "eternity with God." We can understand what Jesus is telling us when He said to all seven churches, "He that hath an ear, let him hear what the Spirit saith unto the churches" (Revelation 2:7, 11, 17, 29; 3:6, 13, 22). It is apparent that our Lord was emphasizing the urgency for us to understand the importance of listening attentively to what the Holy Spirit desires to tell us.

We live in a world that is inundated with television, radio, newspaper, magazine, and talk show opinions, as well as political rhetoric and overwhelming information from the Internet and elsewhere. Our ears are constantly being bombarded with everything from constant cell phone conversations to telemarketing sales pitches, new age philosophy, and messages about the urgent need for change, and the list continues to grow. It seems to me that the only one who isn't changing is God! He said, "I change not" (Malachi 3:6). Also, it appears to me that God is the only one we aren't listening to. If we aren't very careful, we will have our ears and minds filled with everything except what the Holy Spirit wants to tell us. Two relevant questions are: Are we a good listener? Are we listening to the right person and the right things?

The Greek word for ear is *ous*, which is defined as "the faculty of perceiving with the mind, the faculty of understanding and knowing."[15] In Romans 12:2, Paul tells us, "be not conformed to this world: but be ye transformed by the renewing of your mind, that ye may prove what is that good, and acceptable, and perfect, will of God." Paul states in Philippians 2:5, "Let this mind be in you, which was also in Christ Jesus." If we aren't attentive to the Holy Spirit, we can easily be swayed like a reed to believe every wind of doctrine blowing throughout the United States, and, in fact, throughout the earth today (see 2 Timothy 3:1–7 and 4:3–4).

I believe "renewing our mind" occurs as we trust and let the Holy Spirit guide us, on a continual basis. Remember that God's Word teaches us, "to be carnally minded is death; but to be spiritually minded is life and peace. Because the carnal mind is enmity against God" (Romans 8:6–7). Doesn't it make you more joyous, happy, and at peace to listen and follow the Holy Spirit's leadership and to know the fleshly appetites that try to constantly bombard our carnal minds will one day be done away with. This will happen when "all who are in Christ Jesus" get to heaven. In that eternal day we will have the mind of Christ forever, for we will be eternally in His presence. Only then all the former things that have caused us pain, heartache, stress, and despair will have passed away, forever (Revelation 21:4). What a blessed thought!

Heaven includes a new earth and the new Jerusalem. Our minds can't begin to comprehend the beauty and splendor of God's City of Gold, with its wall of jasper, twelve gates of pearl, twelve foundations garnished with twelve precious stones and the Street of Gold (possibly running in twelve directions and connecting to the twelve entrances to the new Jerusalem). To enjoy all of this and the tree of life, river of life, and much, much more will be awesome. That will be an eternal day where the Lamb (Jesus) is the Light, and we, the bride of Christ, will live with Him in heavenly bliss.

Just think: God made man in His image—after His likeness—for His good pleasure and has prepared His city for His bride to live with Him in His presence, serving God and the Lamb forever. In the chapters that follow, we will discuss the above, tour the Holy City, and illustrate "what if" scenarios as we continue our "Sights and Sounds" journey.

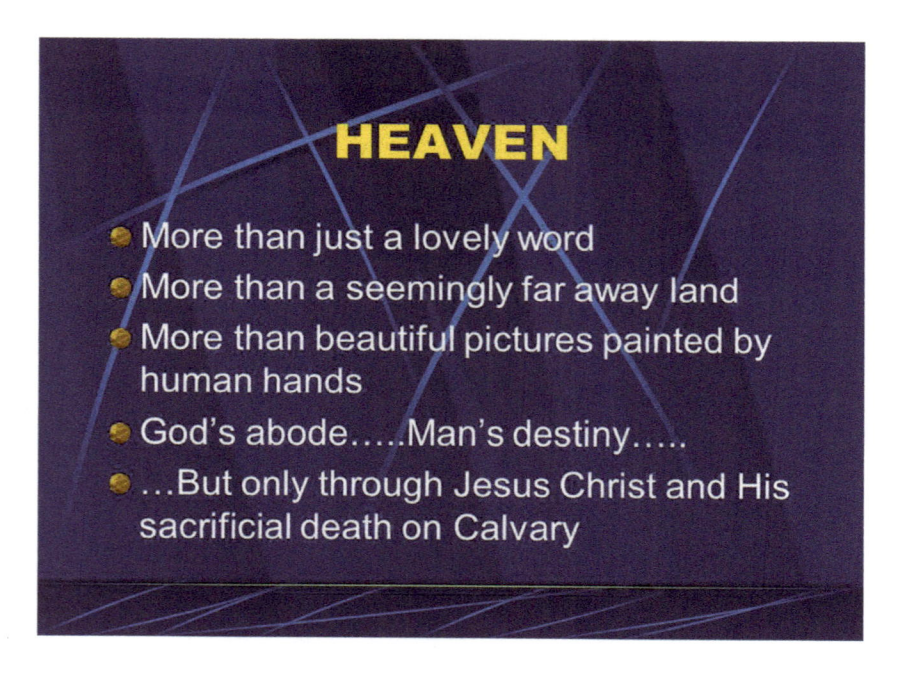

HEAVEN

- More than just a lovely word
- More than a seemingly far away land
- More than beautiful pictures painted by human hands
- God's abode…..Man's destiny…..
- …But only through Jesus Christ and His sacrificial death on Calvary

CHAPTER III

NAMES OF THE CITY OF GOD

The Bible contains many names for God's house, and I have listed several (with references) in the following graphic. You may find others by searching the Scriptures, which is a good spiritual exercise. Of course, we all love to read and hear Jesus telling His disciples (and us), "In my Father's house are many mansions" (John 14:2). The word *many* is defined as "several, a great number, abundance, much, etc." However, it also means "diversity and variety."[16] I believe Jesus has gone to prepare different types of mansions (places, rooms), and the décor will, without a doubt, be exceedingly beautiful. I think His Father's house is the new Jerusalem and includes various architectural styles and designs for the mansions, as well as colors and furnishings. Why do I believe this? Although God made all men and women in His image and after His likeness, we all look different, come in different shapes and sizes, and have different colors of skin, hair, and eyes. We like different clothing styles and colors, and we have different DNA and fingerprints. It appears to me that God loves variety and diversity; we human beings would be more comfortable with one another if we learned this as well.

Names of the City of God

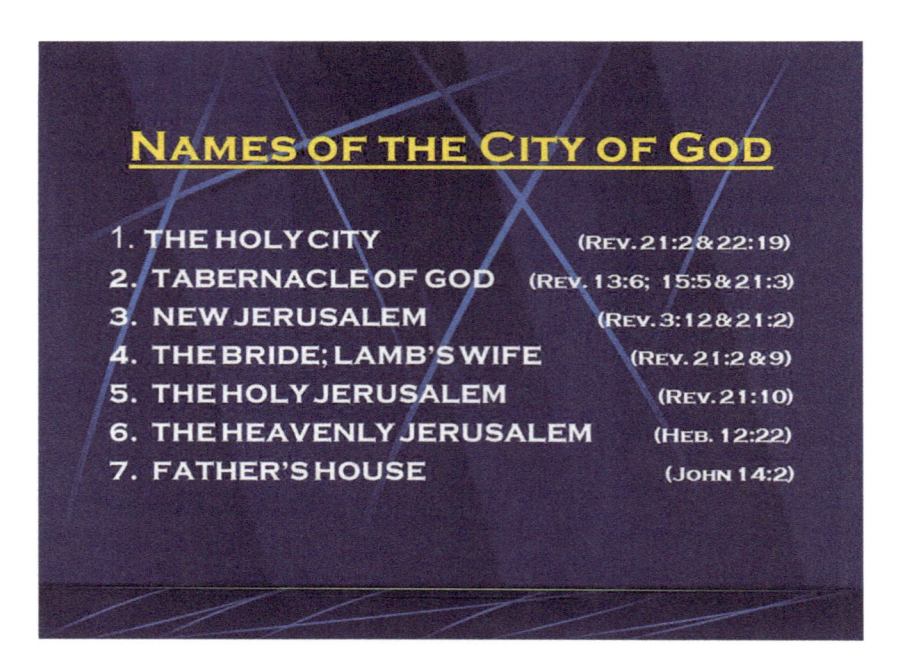

1. THE HOLY CITY (Rev. 21:2 & 22:19)
2. TABERNACLE OF GOD (Rev. 13:6; 15:5 & 21:3)
3. NEW JERUSALEM (Rev. 3:12 & 21:2)
4. THE BRIDE; LAMB'S WIFE (Rev. 21:2 & 9)
5. THE HOLY JERUSALEM (Rev. 21:10)
6. THE HEAVENLY JERUSALEM (Heb. 12:22)
7. FATHER'S HOUSE (John 14:2)

Heaven's Newness

Jesus, as Alpha (the first) and Omega (the last), says, "Behold, I make all things *new*" (Revelation 21:5 emphasis added). The Greek word for *new* is *kainos*. In this passage of Scripture, the word *new* has a different meaning than we are accustomed to. We may buy a new car, a new house, or new clothes, but the newness quickly wears out or gets old. When Jesus uses the word *kainos*, He means "unused, unworn."[17] In other words, the new Jerusalem will be "forever new." Remember the great hymn, "Where We'll Never Grow Old"; those words will surely ring true in the new Jerusalem.

"NEVER GROW OLD"[18]

Verse I
I have heard of a land on the faraway strand,
'Tis a beautiful home of the soul;
Built by Jesus on high, where we never shall die,
'Tis a land where we never grow old.

Refrain
Never grow old, never grow old,
In a land where we'll never grow old;
Never grow old, never grow old,
In a land where we'll never grow old.

Verse II
In that beautiful home where we'll never more roam,
We shall be in the sweet by and by;
Happy praise to the King through eternity sing,
'Tis a land where we never shall die.

Verse III
When our work here is done and the life-crown is won,
And our troubles and trials are o'er;
All our sorrow will end, and our voices will blend,
With the loved ones who've gone on before.

James C. Moore (1914, public domain)

RONNIE S. KENNETT

Heaven's Newness: The Children of Israel—Their Clothes, Shoes, Food, and Drink

I am reminded of the children of Israel as Moses led them through the wilderness for forty years. We are told that this journey could have taken only eleven days, yet God patiently listened to their murmuring and complaining so much that He saw to it that they journeyed forty years.

Consider how the Lord watched over two million to three million Israelites (so we are told) wandering in this vast wilderness, and how He fed them with manna (heavenly food) and quail (earthly food), gave them water (sometimes from a rock), clothed them, kept shoes on their feet, and saw to it that Moses led them until he died and Joshua took over leadership.

Deuteronomy 29:5 tells us that the children of Israel's *clothes* didn't wax old (*remained new*), and their shoes didn't wax old (that means *remained new* to me), and although they had to do many, many miles of walking, their feet didn't swell (wow!). (See Deuteronomy 8:4.) Yes, God once again showed His miracle-working power, didn't He? Remember, they were having children, growing older, dying, etc., and yet, God took care of them with clothing and shoes amid their continual murmuring and complaining. I don't know, but I suppose you could say they wore *new* hand-me-down clothes and shoes and saw to it that their children and grandchildren did so as well for forty years. In addition, Deuteronomy 29:6 tells us, "Ye have not eaten bread, neither have ye drunk wine or strong drink: that ye might know that I am the Lord thy God." It is clear to me that the children of Israel did not drink any alcoholic beverages for forty years.

SIGHTS AND SOUNDS OF HEAVEN

SEVEN NEW THINGS
Rev. 21

1. NEW HEAVEN
2. NEW EARTH
3. NEW JERUSALEM
4. NEW PEOPLES
5. NEW TEMPLE
6. NEW LIGHT
7. NEW PARADISE

Listed on the preceding graphic are seven new things mentioned in Revelation 21. First, John saw a new heaven. Second Peter 3:10 tells us, "the (current) heavens shall pass away with a great noise...," and Isaiah 65:17 states, "For, behold, I create *new heavens* and a *new earth*...." Next, John sees the new earth spoken of by the prophet Isaiah. In Matthew 24:35, Mark 13:31, and Luke 21:33, Jesus said, "Heaven and earth shall pass away: but My Words shall not pass away." Also, we are told that the earth abideth forever, meaning this old earth will be made over new. The new earth will be free from all impurities created by sin and the devil.

John then sees the new Jerusalem coming down from God out of heaven. The earthly Jerusalem has served its purpose through the millennial reign of Jesus and is no more. God replaces it with the eternal new Jerusalem. This city will house the bride, the Lamb's wife. They are clothed in robes of linen, clean and white, without spot and blemish, and they have come from every nation on this earth, and from every kindred and tongue. It is overwhelming to read about the "heroes of faith" in Hebrews 11 and to meditate on worshiping our Lord with the patriarchs of old, the apostles of the Lamb, our loved ones, friends and all who have died in the faith. What a glorious day that will be!

There will not be a temple in the new Jerusalem, for the city itself will be the most holy place, and God and the Lamb will be the temple thereof (Revelation 21:22). There will not be a need for a wilderness tabernacle, Solomon's temple, the New Testament temples, or a tribulation and millennium temple anymore.

There will be a new light. Revelation 21:23 states, "And the city had no need of the sun, neither of the moon, to shine in it: for the glory of God did lighten it, and the Lamb is the light thereof." John beheld something more beautiful and glorious than even the garden of Eden. Truly, the new Jerusalem will be a New Paradise. I haven't traveled extensively, and even though we have some beautiful places on earth, these worldly paradises, probably including the garden of Eden, can't begin to compare with the new heaven, new earth, and the new Jerusalem.

A New Name

Have you given thought concerning the new name that Jesus will give each one in heaven? When Jesus speaks to the angel of the church of Pergamos, He promises each of us a white stone with a new name in it. Jesus, as Alpha and Omega, says, "To him that overcometh will I give to eat of the hidden manna, and will give him a white stone, and in the stone a new name written, which no man knoweth saving he that receiveth it" (Revelation 2:17). He tells the angel of the Philadelphia church, "Him that overcometh will I make a pillar in the temple of my God, and he shall go no more in or out: and I will write upon him the name of my God, and the name of the city of my God, which is new Jerusalem, which cometh down out of heaven from my God: and I will write upon him my new name" (Revelation 3:12).

I must confess that I do not have any tattoos on me, and I am not one who caters to the tattoo customs that are prevalent in today's society. Also, I like my name, Ronnie Sherwood Kennett, since my mother and father gave it to me. Mom would often remind me that my name is Ronnie, not Ronald. Many people like their names, some say they don't like their name, and others have had their names changed for various reasons. I've talked to people who wish they had never been tattooed and some who like their tattoo(s). I don't read in God's Word where there will be any tattoos in heaven (no offense); however, I am sure of one thing: when Jesus writes new names on us, it will be wonderful and glorious to receive them and wear them.

A New Song

When John sees the twenty-four elders in Revelation 4, they are clothed in "white raiment" and sitting on seats, wearing crowns of gold. They bow before the throne, worshipping God and the Lamb, and cast their crowns before the throne. These elders represent the redeemed of both the Old and New Testaments: twelve for the tribes of Israel and twelve for the apostles. In Revelation 4:11, they say (they may be singing, as we do today), "Thou art worthy, O Lord, to receive glory and honour and power: for thou hast created all things, and for thy pleasure they are and were created." Later, they fall down before the Lamb and sing a new song, saying,

> Thou art worthy to take the book, and to open the seals thereof: for thou wast slain, and hast redeemed us to God by thy blood, out of every kindred, and

tongue, and people, and nation; and hast made us unto our God kings and priests: and we shall reign on the earth.(Revelation 5:9–10)

CLEARLY THIS IS A NEW SONG OF ONLY THE REDEEMED.

In Revelation 14:3, the 144,000 sing a new song that no one else can sing. We are not told why others cannot join them in this song, but I am sure it will be a beautiful and glorious "sight and sound." Chapter 15 tells us that those who have been saved, and probably were martyred, during the great tribulation will stand on the "sea of glass" and sing the song of Moses and the song of the Lamb. They will sing,

> Great and marvelous art thy works, Lord God Almighty; just and true are thy ways, thou King of saints. Who shall not fear thee, O Lord, and glorify thy name? for thou only art holy: for all nations shall come and worship before thee; for thy judgments are made manifest.(Revelation 15: 3–4)

It is very appropriate that we will sing *new songs* in heaven, since everything there will be new.

I am really looking forward to singing in heaven's choir, aren't you? I have been privileged to lead choirs and congregations in singing over the years, as well as being a choir member. And, who can ever forget those Billy Graham choirs led by Cliff Barrows? However, as wonderful as singing praises to God and the Lamb has been here, nothing will compare to the "sights and sounds" of heaven's choir joining in the song of the redeemed, which even the angels cannot sing. That song is reserved for all who are redeemed by and through the precious, royal blood of our risen Savior and Lord, Jesus Christ. In a future chapter I will elaborate further on this "heavenly music" (Revelation 5:8–10).[19]

Since we are discussing heavenly music, I believe it is appropriate for me to insert a song I wrote in 1986 which follows:

"Step Up to Meet Jesus"[20]

Verse I
Jesus Christ, the Son of God, virgin born on earth did trod,
He died upon the rugged cross our sins to bear.
He arose on the third day; His disciples saw him go away.
When He returns, I'll rise to meet Him in the air.

Refrain
Then I'll step up to meet Jesus in the air,
I won't have to put on wings, I won't need to pray a prayer.
All my battles will be done, a crown of victory will be won,
When I step up to meet Jesus in the air.

Verse II
This world we're living in today, full of sin and disarray,
Many souls, it seems, are sinking in despair.
It takes the blood of Christ applied and the love of God inside,
If we expect to meet Jesus in the air.

Words and music by Ronnie S. Kennett

A New Body

Have you taken a close look at yourself recently? The houses of clay that we live in are decaying, aren't they? I enjoy asking audiences if they have looked closely at themselves in the mirror today. Even though we may have plastic surgery, tummy tucks, facials, haircuts, and the like, just a glance at ourselves should remind us often that someday these bodies will decay. I am not a gloom and doom person;

however, God's word assures us, "it is appointed unto men once to die, but after this the judgment" (Hebrews 9:27). If we have accepted Jesus Christ as Savior, we will have a new celestial body fashioned like our Lord's own glorious body (Philippians 3:21). Hallelujah! If I have said that already, it bears repeating. Jesus, who will outshine everything in heaven, has promised us that we shall be like Him. While we see through a glass darkly now, we shall soon see Him face-to-face and live with Him eternally, in bodies that will never, never grow old (1 Corinthians 13:12 and 15:44). This is a blessed hope!

Paul compares our heavenly bodies to our earthly bodies (1 Corinthians 15:42–44). Realizing that these temples of clay will decay and return to dust, it is good for us to remind ourselves of Paul's exhortation that follows:

Earthly Body	Heavenly Body
Sown in corruption	Raised in incorruption
Sown in dishonor	Raised in glory
Sown in weakness	Raised in power
Sown a natural body	Raised a spiritual body

When we think of the spiritual body we will have in heaven, it is important to remember that our body will be fashioned like Jesus' glorious body. After His resurrection, Jesus could walk through a wall or closed door; He could be touched and He could eat; He appeared and vanished at will, and over five hundred witnesses of His resurrection saw him before His ascension. Although we cannot comprehend our glorious spiritual body, we know it will be tangible, since we will know as we are known, we will eat and drink, we will walk and talk, and we will worship, praise, and serve God and the Lamb forever.

We should be happy and rejoicing that God has such a perfect plan, purpose, and design for His children.

As illustrated above, our earthly body will be sown in weakness but raised in power, and forever we will live with our Lord in His heavenly paradise in our new bodies. And remember, the bride of Christ will inherit and enjoy their new bodies at Jesus' second coming. Wow! Doesn't that mean we will break them in during the millennial reign and enjoy them forever in heaven with Jesus eternally?

A NEW LIFE

Revelation 21:4 says,

> And God shall wipe away all tears from their eyes;
> and there shall be no more death, neither sorrow,
> nor crying, neither shall there be any more pain: for
> the former things are passed away.

Wow! Have we really paused to think about our new bodies and the new life we will enjoy in heaven? Consider, with me, just some of the many things of this earthly life that *won't* be present in heaven:

- No sickness or disease, which means no broken-down bodies crippled with arthritis, polio, etc.
- No cancer, heart disease, or other dreaded diseases.
- No doctors, nurses, hospitals, medicines, pharmacies, or—you name it. These have served us on earth but won't be needed in heaven.

- No murder, abortions, child abuse, family disagreements, marrying, or giving in marriage.
- No church denominations, splits, or divisions.
- No death, which means no sorrow or deathbed scenes, corpses, coffins, hearses, graves, funeral homes, pallbearers, sad songs, or grieving.
- No growing old, which means no Alzheimer's disease or nursing, convalescent, or assisted-living homes.
- No more praying, only praising God and the Lamb—forever.
- No taxes or stimulus packages and no need for money in any form, which means no worry over unpaid bills, no banks, Wall Street, economic concerns, thieves, or robbers.
- No wars or rumors of wars.
- No nuclear warheads.
- No malice or strife.
- No fear.
- No more night. The list is endless.

MORE NEW THINGS

- **NEW NAME**
  Rev. 2:17 & 3:12
- **NEW SONG**
  Rev. 5:9 & 14:3
- **NEW BODY**
  Philippians 3:20-21
- **NEW LIFE**
  Rev. 22:5

"For the former things are passed away" (Revelation 21:4)! Why do I list some of the above? Because, there will be *no more sin* and *no more devil*. "For the former things are passed away"! *How beautiful heaven will be*!

An Imperfect Earth and a Perfect Heaven

As I write this section, the unemployment rate of the United States is estimated to be between 4.5% and 5%. Many of citizens of the United States are without jobs, and the actual unemployment numbers and percentages are probably twice as high as reported by the media. We wrestle with this dilemma and other problems that seemingly appear insoluble. In addition, over the last few years, our government has been rapidly changing laws that conform to insatiable appetites that feed sinful pleasure, power, and greed. No consideration has been given to God's Word, on which our nation was founded. There is no question or doubt in my mind that we are nearing the time when Jesus shall return, and the rapture of His church will take place.

Sadly, many who once attended church regularly, took time to pray, and freely devoted time and talents to ministry have either turned away from assembling together in worship or no longer find time to serve God. If they do attend a church, they do not want to be committed to serving in any position, desire no active participation in church services, and want sermons that satisfy their fleshly desires. Many search portions of Scripture to find *private* interpretations that will fit their agendas or beliefs. The apostle Peter warned us clearly: "Knowing this first, that no prophecy of any scripture is of private interpretation" (2 Peter 1:20). The word *prophecy* means "divinely-empowered forthtelling (asserting the mind of God) or foretelling (prediction)."[21]

RONNIE S. KENNETT

In the 1980s I stumbled upon a list of earthly imperfections that require perfect remedies. As I recall, this list originated in an article entitled "Walking with the King."[22] It certainly highlights that Jesus Christ is the only answer for the many dilemmas facing all humanity in our imperfect world today. As you will see, this list is sobering, but we have the answer in the only perfect person to walk on this earth.

I Am That I Am

Remember the time when an angel of the Lord appeared to Moses "in a flame of fire out of the midst of a burning bush" (Exodus 3:2–13).

A painting titled *The Burning Bush* by artist Pat Marvenko Smith illustrates what Moses saw and is pictured above.

- "And God said unto Moses, 'I AM THAT I AM': And He said, 'Thus shalt thou say unto the children of Israel, "I AM" hath sent me unto you'" (Exodus 3:14).
- God mentions His name, "I AM," in the Old Testament, and then He reveals His name, "I AM," through His Son, Jesus Christ, in the New Testament.

Lord (Jehovah) God

- He that is who He is.
- The self-existent one: literally, the eternal "I AM" ...
- I AM: the self-existent one who reveals himself...

JESUS IS THE GREAT I AM

- Jesus is our sustenance: "I AM the bread of life" (John 6:35)
- Jesus is our source: "I AM the light of the world" (John 8:12; 9:5)
- Jesus is our salvation: "I AM the door" (John 10:7, 9 and Revelation 3:20)
- Jesus is our shepherd: "I AM the Good Shepherd" (John 10:11)
- Jesus is our Sustainer: "I AM the Resurrection and the Life" (John 11:25 and 26)
- Jesus is our Supplier: "I AM the True Vine" (John 15:4 and 5)

- Jesus is our Secret Place: "I AM the Way, the Truth, and the Life" (John 14:6)
- Jesus is our Sonshine (sunshine): "I AM the Alpha and Omega (Revelation 1:8)

Yes! Jesus is:

- Heaven's bread for earth's hunger
- Heaven's cure for earth's curse
- Heaven's life for earth's death
- Heaven's light for earth's darkness
- Heaven's blessing for earth's blight
- Heaven's remedy for earth's disease
- Heaven's water for earth's thirst
- Heaven's grace for earth's guilt
- Heaven's sunshine for earth's shadow
- Heaven's fullness for earth's emptiness
- Heaven's eternity for earth's short day
- Heaven's mercy for earth's misery
- Heaven's salvation for earth's sin
- Heaven's redemption for earth's ruin
- Heaven's *love* for earth's hatred

Yes, the former things of this earth will all have passed away. Everything will be made new. Someone once said something that it is so, so true: "Jesus said it, I believe it, and that settles it."[24] What a new life we will enjoy forever and ever in heaven!

SIGHTS AND SOUNDS OF HEAVEN

CHAPTER IV

NEWNESS: NAMES, SONGS, BODIES

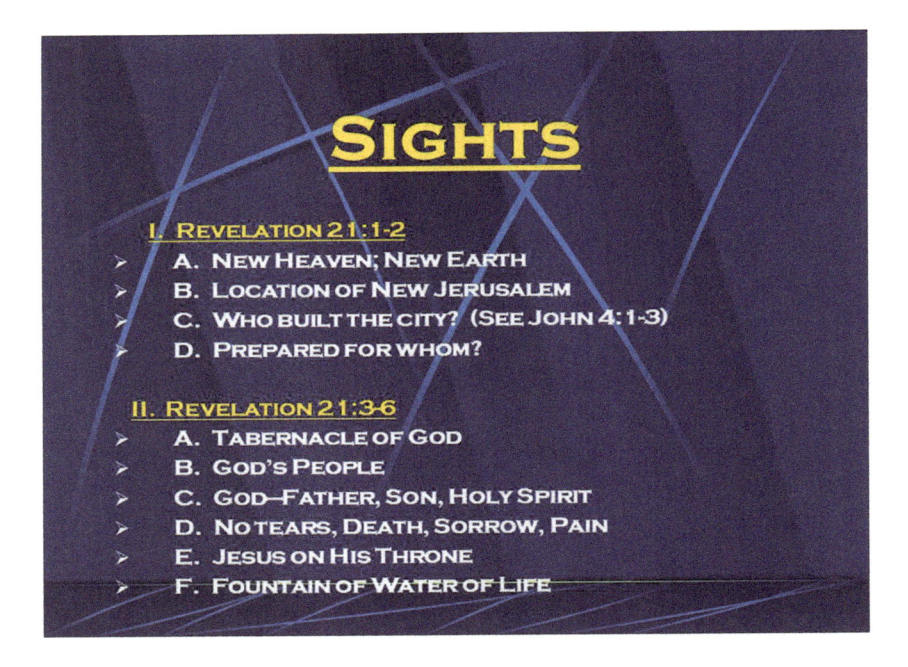

SIGHTS

I. Revelation 21:1-2
- A. New Heaven; New Earth
- B. Location of New Jerusalem
- C. Who built the city? (See John 4:1-3)
- D. Prepared for whom?

II. Revelation 21:3-6
- A. Tabernacle of God
- B. God's People
- C. God—Father, Son, Holy Spirit
- D. No Tears, Death, Sorrow, Pain
- E. Jesus on His Throne
- F. Fountain of Water of Life

The apostle John's first ten words in Revelation 21:1 are: "*And I saw a new heaven and a new earth*: for the first heaven and the first earth were passed away; and there was no more sea" (emphasis added).

Heavenly Sights and Sounds Overview

Now that we have glimpses of the newness of the new Jerusalem, let us turn our attention to an overview of what we will *discuss in detail* in later chapters. Revelation chapters 21 and 22 give the setting. There is a new heaven and a new earth, the new Jerusalem descending out of heaven, the master builder of this city and those for whom it has been prepared. We'll discuss this tabernacle of God, Jesus, as Alpha and Omega, sitting on His throne, the fountain of water of life and the angel giving John a bird's-eye view of the new Jerusalem's splendor and beauty.

This beloved apostle describes the city of gold and its light, the city wall, the gates, the wall foundations, and the throne. I'm sure John marveled at the size of the city and wall and the breathtaking view of the street of gold, the river of life, and the tree of life. Can you imagine John's worship and praise as he envisions the nations walking in the light of that city and the kings of the new earth bringing the glory and honor of the nations into the new Jerusalem to present them to God the Father and the Lamb (Jesus)? Yes, John beholds the Lamb, Jesus Christ, our Savior and Lord, sitting on His throne, and although John had walked with Jesus on earth and fell at His feet (Revelation 1:17), perhaps, in heaven, we will hear him share just how he felt at that moment. Come to think of it, I wonder how you and I will feel when we see Jesus in this setting.

In addition, listen with me to some of the sounds on which we will be focusing our spiritual ears. I believe we will hear God's voice, comforting and powerfully soothing—there is none greater. And, as Alpha and Omega, Jesus speaks, perhaps as the sound of many waters (see Revelation 1:15). Can you hear the angel as he informs John of all he is seeing and hearing? It will surely be wonderful to hear these voices audibly in heaven, after we hear, "Come up hither," from Jesus (4:1), won't it? Oh yes, put your hand behind your ear and listen; hear the river of life flowing; the leaves of the tree of life blowing in the breeze of the Holy Spirit; and the people of God worshipping and praising God and the Lamb.

Perhaps the Holy Spirit is inviting you to listen closely to some sounds already? In Revelation 21:3, John "heard a great voice out of heaven saying, 'Behold, the tabernacle of God is with men, and He will dwell with them, and they shall be His people, and God Himself shall be with them, and be their God.'" I believe this is God's voice. Then in Revelation 21:4, we learn that "God shall wipe away all tears from their eyes; and there shall be no more death, neither sorrow, nor crying, neither shall there be any more pain: for the former things are passed away."

Then Jesus, the Alpha and Omega, speaks, declaring,

> Behold, I make all things new...Write: for these words are true and faithful.... I am Alpha and Omega, the beginning and the end. I will give unto him that is athirst of the fountain of the water of life freely. He that overcometh shall inherit all things; and I will be his God, and he shall be my son. (Revelation 21:5–7).

I am so grateful to have this opportunity to share with you in this book what God has burned within my heart about heaven and the new Jerusalem and some of the sights and sounds that await His children.

I have already included a few songs I have written over the years, and I believe their words are relevant today. In addition, I am inserting other songs that I consider appropriate. One such song is titled:

RONNIE S. KENNETT

"The Old, Old Story"[26]

Verse I
I love to hear the old, old story,
About Jesus who came to save us from sin.
How he was born of the Virgin Mary,
And with his disciples, He walked among men.
I love to hear how He cleansed the lepers,
Healed disease and sickness, He opened blind eyes.
He made the cripple to walk, the deaf to hear, the dumb to talk,
And His bride will rise to meet Him when He splits the eastern skies.

Refrain
Jesus may come today without warning;
He may come in the morning, at night or at noon.
But there is one thing I know, beyond a shadow of a doubt.
Jesus Christ, our redeemer, is coming very soon.

Verse II
I love to tell of God's wonderful mercy,
Jesus died on the cross to redeem us from sin.
Then He arose from the tomb on the third day,
And ascended with this promise, I will come back again.

Verse III
I love to talk about the beauties of heaven.
The mansions and the place Jesus went to prepare.
The gates of pearl, the street of gold,
The bride of Christ, we'll never grow old.
And the Lamb will be the light of that city foursquare.

Words and music by Ronnie S. Kennett

SOUNDS

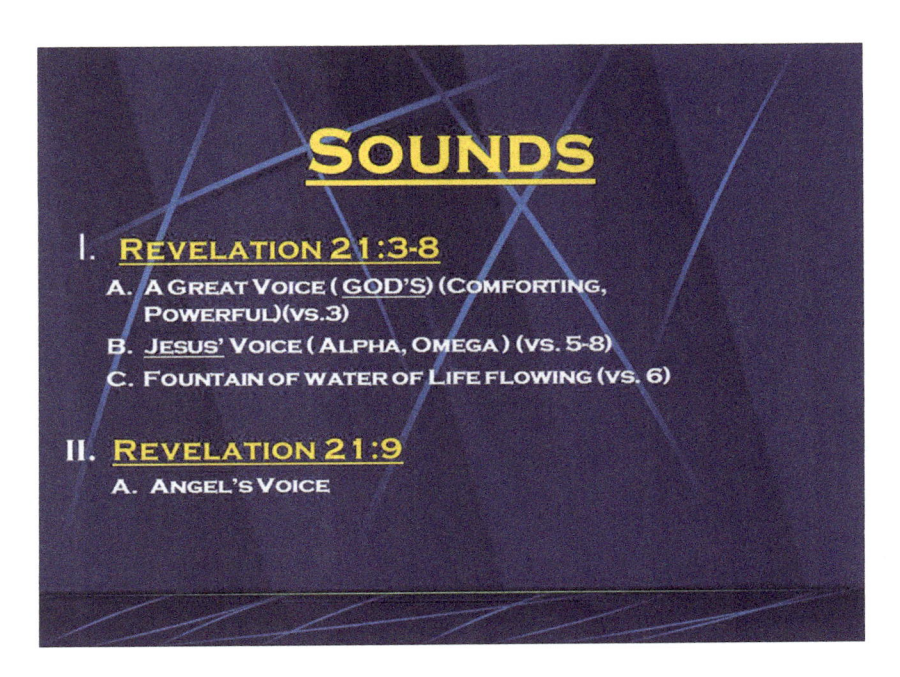

I. **REVELATION 21:3-8**
   A. A GREAT VOICE (GOD'S) (COMFORTING, POWERFUL) (VS. 3)
   B. JESUS' VOICE (ALPHA, OMEGA) (VS. 5-8)
   C. FOUNTAIN OF WATER OF LIFE FLOWING (VS. 6)

II. **REVELATION 21:9**
   A. ANGEL'S VOICE

THE CITY OF GOD

Revelation 21:1–2 says,

> *And I saw a new heaven and a new earth*: for the first heaven and the first earth were passed away; and there was no more sea. And I John saw the holy city, new Jerusalem, coming down from God out of heaven, prepared as a bride adorned for her husband. (emphasis added).

I love these words, and the fact that John writes what he saw in the first person. Did you notice? John uses his name for the second time during his writings. Previously, he had written the New Testament Gospel of John along with First, Second, and Third John, yet in those he never mentioned his own name. He does not write it until Revelation 1:9 and then again in Revelation 21. I suggest John was so enthused and overwhelmed by what he saw and heard that he wanted everyone who reads these words to comprehend his personal emotions, as well as how glorious those "Sights and Sounds" will be when we see and hear them.

John begins to relate what he saw personally in the Spirit. He describes a city of gold, as transparent glass, which I believe is suspended above the earth. Wow! He tells how the angel takes him to a high mountain to view the city, which is called the bride.

Why does John call the new Jerusalem the bride, the Lamb's wife? First, because Jesus Christ has taken His bride unto Himself in Revelation 19:7–9, and after the marriage supper of the Lamb has taken place, Jesus has presented this perfect new abiding place to His bride. I believe that while the first heaven and first earth are being dissolved and made over new, and the new heaven(s) and new earth are being prepared, the Bridegroom and His bride will be living in this new Jerusalem and will do so forever. This vision John saw is clearly set forth in Revelation 21:9–10 when the angel takes him to behold the bride, the Lamb's wife, and the apostle sees the holy Jerusalem, descending out of heaven from God. To me, there is no indication that new Jerusalem is setting *on* the earth.

Keep in mind that John has already seen the visible new Jerusalem descending from God, out of heaven (Rev 21:1–2). I believe the angel shows the city to John a second time in detail to emphasize that the Bridegroom and His bride (wife) are housed in the holy city. Lastly, God and Jesus, as the Lamb, are the light and the temple of the new Jerusalem. The nations of the earth will walk in the light of that city, and the kings of the earth will bring the glory and honor of the nations of the new earth into the eternal, holy Jerusalem forever.

While I respect the views of those who see the new Jerusalem as the bride and not as a visible city, I do not. I see the new Jerusalem as a literal city for the reasons stated herein. The following graphics illustrate such setting.

27

RONNIE S. KENNETT

Since I believe the new Jerusalem will be a visible city, section II of *Sights and Sounds of Heaven* will include some earthly comparisons to my thoughts about heaven and the pearly white city. Perhaps you may compare other cities as well.

SECTION II

EARTHLY COMPARISONS WITH NEW JERUSALEM

CHAPTER V

COMPARING THE EARTHLY JERUSALEM WITH THE NEW JERUSALEM

The earthly Jerusalem is the largest city in Israel, and its population in 2008 totaled approximately 850,000. The city's area is approximately 48.3 square miles. Two temples have been built in Jerusalem, and both were destroyed.[28] A third temple will be built in the (near) future, and Jesus will rule from that temple in Jerusalem for one thousand years, during His millennial reign on earth. By the way, His church (the bride) will reign with Him.

JERUSALEM'S WHITE LIMESTONE

An interesting fact regarding Jerusalem is the composition of some of its buildings today. White limestone is being used to build many of the city's structures, and in the afternoon sun, this white limestone reflects light with a golden hue. History records that this mysterious layer of white limestone wasn't found until King Solomon began building the first temple almost three thousand years ago. Geologically, we are told, this white limestone is so soft that before it is exposed to the air, it can be chiseled easily by masons to make perfectly square-sized blocks to use in building temples, palaces, etc.[29]

We can readily see that the forty-eight square mile area of the earthly Jerusalem doesn't begin to compare to the 2,250,000 square miles of the new Jerusalem. There will be no need for a temple in the new Jerusalem, for God and the Lamb will be the temple of that city. The new Jerusalem will be a city of gold as transparent glass.

It is interesting to note that the earthly Jerusalem is known as the center of the earth, and, I believe, without doubt, the new Jerusalem will be the central focal point and capital of the new heaven and new earth for eternity. The nations of the new earth and everything in the new heaven and the new earth will focus on Jesus Christ, our Savior and Lord. What a Savior, what a city, and what an eternal day we will enjoy in heaven!

Heavenly Time

I have been asked many times, "Ronnie, what will we be doing in heaven for all eternity?" That is an easy question to answer. We will be worshipping and serving God and the Lamb, Jesus, forever (Revelation 22:3–5). After all, we have established the fact that eternity is timeless, since Jehovah Elohim, our Creator, is timeless, and, in heaven we will no longer be living on *chronos* (Greek), or earthly time. We will live forever on *kairos* (Greek), or God's time. Just think—no more clocks or watches, no more timetables or earthly schedules. By the way, shouldn't we devote more of our earthly time to proclaiming the Gospel of Jesus Christ to this lost and dying world while we have time? I once heard that a Christian should be like a good watch: pure gold, open faced, well regulated, always on time, and full of good works. Hmmmm... have you taken time today to tell someone about Jesus?

Having touched on heavenly and earthly time, I wonder many times if I could have spent my time more wisely at home, at work, and sharing much less chronos time concentrating on earthly things and more kairos time. After all, while we need money on earth to take care of our families, we will not need earthly things at all in heaven, will we?

My mind goes back to 1981 when I was watching CBS News with reporter Charles Osgood. He caught my attention by presenting a poem, which I have kept over the years and have used from time to time, as follows:

"THE BILLION DOLLAR POEM"[30]

When you think of a number,
as numbers are reckoned,
consider a billion in minutes and seconds.
Consider that two billion seconds ago,
the a-bomb had not been exploded, you know.

So a billion of anything, that's a whole lot,
we know it of course, but we really do not.
Two billion minutes, how much time is that worth,
that long ago Christ was still walking on earth.

Two billion minutes ago, if you count,
Jesus was giving his sermon up there on the mount.
And one billion hours, the time men were slaves,
a billion hours ago men were living in caves.

continued

RONNIE S. KENNETT

Here's a statistic that should give you warning,
our government spent over seven billion dollars since
yesterday morning.
Yes, that's how much money our government spent,
just to give you an idea of how quickly it went.

So, the size a number without any doubt,
just depends on what you're talking about.

> Presented by Charles Osgood on
> CBS News in 1981

CHAPTER VI

NEW JERUSALEM'S SIZE

In Revelation 21:12–21, John describes the new Jerusalem, the bride, and the city of gold, including the wall, the twelve gates, the twelve foundations, and their components. We will explore those later, but in this chapter, let's focus on the size of the city. After you review the following graphics, I will illustrate my perspective of just how vast new Jerusalem is.

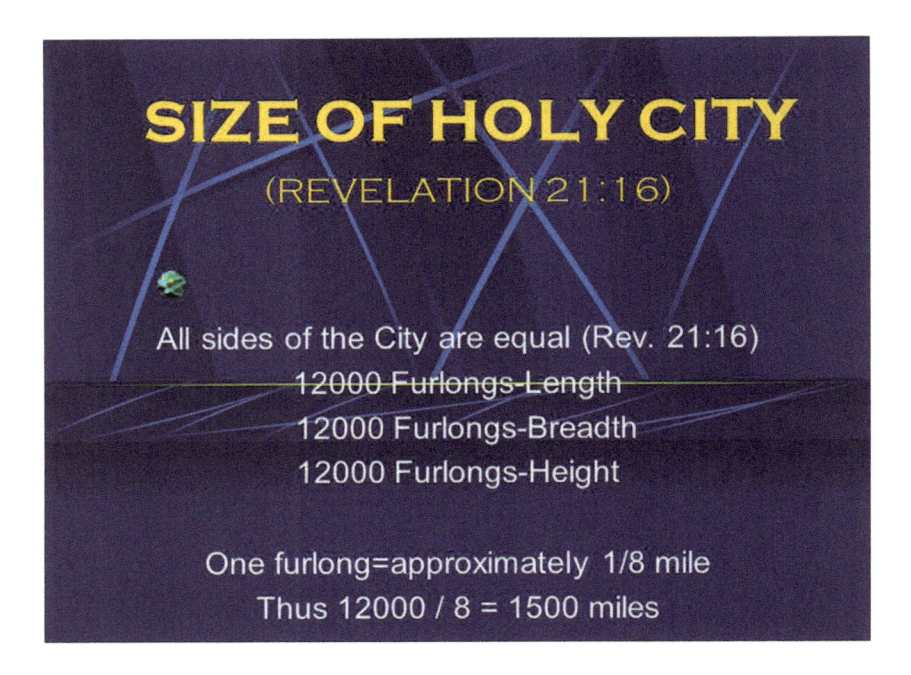

SIZE OF HOLY CITY
(REVELATION 21:16)

All sides of the City are equal (Rev. 21:16)
12000 Furlongs-Length
12000 Furlongs-Breadth
12000 Furlongs-Height

One furlong=approximately 1/8 mile
Thus 12000 / 8 = 1500 miles

SIZE OF HOLY CITY
Revelation 21:16

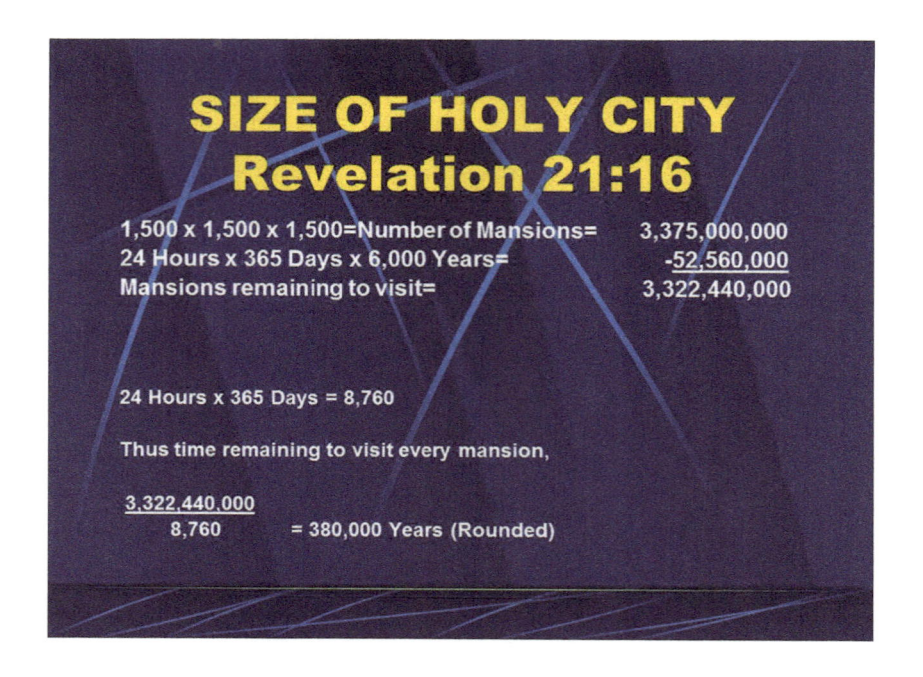

1,500 x 1,500 x 1,500 = Number of Mansions =	3,375,000,000
24 Hours x 365 Days x 6,000 Years =	-52,560,000
Mansions remaining to visit =	3,322,440,000

24 Hours x 365 Days = 8,760

Thus time remaining to visit every mansion,

$$\frac{3,322,440,000}{8,760} = 380,000 \text{ Years (Rounded)}$$

I spent twenty-eight years in banking, and after retiring, I did additional consulting for a while. Also, I have enjoyed working with numbers. Let me illustrate how the size of the new Jerusalem alone proclaims the greatness of our God, while being just a small part of all Jesus promised us when He said, "I go to prepare a place for you" (John 14:1–4).

While some theologians have various theories about the size of the new Jerusalem, I believe, as is illustrated, that the city is 1,500 miles high, wide, and handsome (as my Dad, who is now in heaven, used to say). There are theories that the city will be shaped like a pyramid, with a square base and ascending to a pyramid peak. Personally, I believe the city will be cubical, since Revelation 21:16 clearly states that the length, breadth, and height of it are equal. May I remind you of God's instructions when He gave Solomon the blueprint for the Lord's house (the temple). I Kings 6:20 describes the most holy place, where the ark of the covenant would be housed, to be "And the oracle in the forepart was twenty cubits in length, and twenty cubits in breadth, and twenty cubits in the height thereof: and he overlaid it with pure gold" (or an exact cube).

My "what ifs" are just that. I would never, ever, attempt to add to or take away from God's Word. By using "what if" examples for the number of mansions and the earthly time allotted to visit the mansions, I endeavor to illustrate how huge the new Jerusalem will be and how big our God is. While we do not have any idea of each mansion's size, by using the simple one cubic mile illustration, let me expound on what Jesus said in John 14:1–3. "In my Father's house are many mansions." Surely, there will be many, many mansions in the new Jerusalem, and by definition, they will be diverse in style, colors, décor, etc. We will enjoy eternity serving God and the Lamb and, no doubt, visiting with one another while traveling from mansion to mansion, as well as the expanse of heaven. Therefore, perhaps 3,375,000,000 mansions are not an exaggeration.

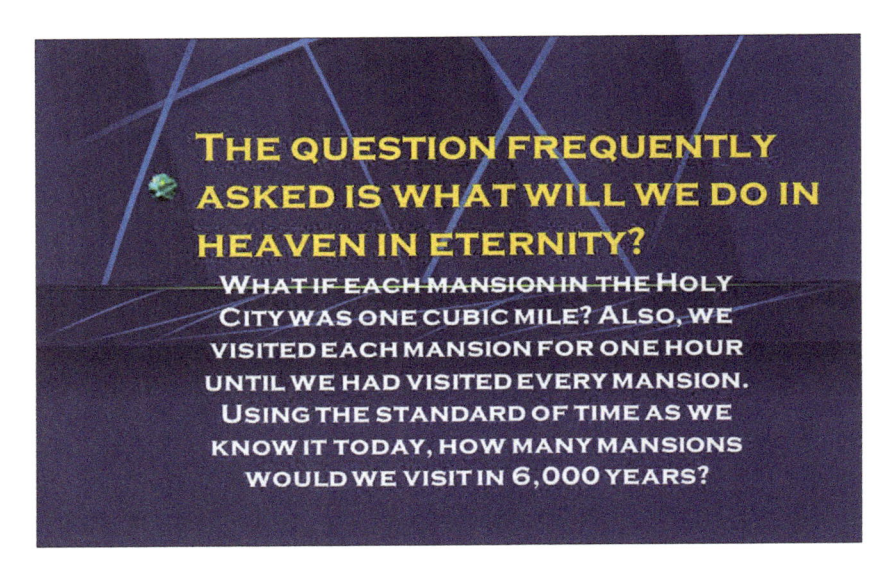

> **THE QUESTION FREQUENTLY ASKED IS WHAT WILL WE DO IN HEAVEN IN ETERNITY?**
> WHAT IF EACH MANSION IN THE HOLY CITY WAS ONE CUBIC MILE? ALSO, WE VISITED EACH MANSION FOR ONE HOUR UNTIL WE HAD VISITED EVERY MANSION. USING THE STANDARD OF TIME AS WE KNOW IT TODAY, HOW MANY MANSIONS WOULD WE VISIT IN 6,000 YEARS?

One of the best examples I have heard regarding a new Jerusalem mansion came during a presentation I did at Cumberland Road

Church of God, in Bluefield, West Virginia, in the early 1990s. My dear friend, Pastor Danny Scott, related a helicopter experience he had with his brother and a coal baron. Danny had been invited to join them for a flight over the coalfields of southwest Virginia. During the flight, Danny's brother began circling a specific area, which continued for some time. Danny became curious about what they were viewing, and his brother informed him they were admiring the very large and beautiful mansion below. Danny spontaneously told them, "That mansion wouldn't even be a doghouse in heaven." I am confident, based solely on God's precious Word, that Danny is right.

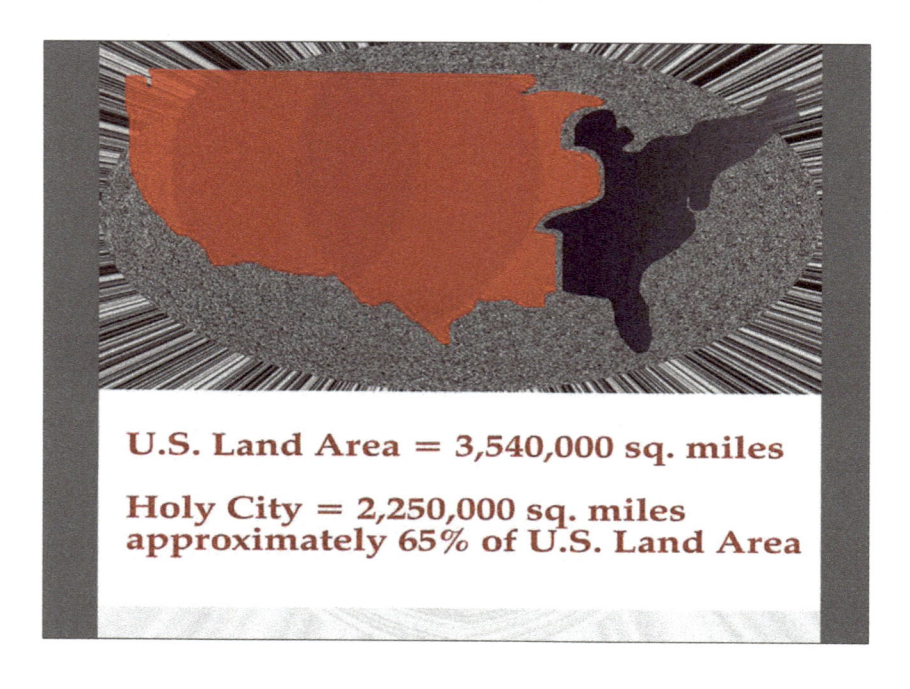

U.S. Land Area = 3,540,000 sq. miles

Holy City = 2,250,000 sq. miles approximately 65% of U.S. Land Area

Let me elaborate on Graphic #20. Notice the red portion of the map of the United States of America. This depicts a "what if." What if the new Jerusalem was setting on an area that equaled the square mile area of the United States of America? Using the square mile scenario

SIGHTS AND SOUNDS OF HEAVEN

and the USA square mile outline map, the holy city could cover approximately 65% of the United States, or 2,250,000 square miles.

To comprehend, to some degree, just how large the new Jerusalem will be, I once read where Dr. Wilbur M. Smith, in his book, *The Biblical Doctrine of Heaven*, gave an insight calculated by an Australian engineer. He estimates the new Jerusalem will be approximately twenty times as big as New Zealand, twenty times as big as Germany, and ten times as big as France. Also, the city will be forty times as big as all of England and even much bigger than India.[31] This emphasizes again just how large the holy city will be.

Space Flight

With 1,500 miles for the new Jerusalem's height, it will rise to more than seven times higher than our astronauts orbit a space shuttle in outer space. My research finds they usually orbit 200 miles to 380 miles above earth. The space station is orbiting at 240 miles, high and the Hubble telescope orbits at 380 miles above the earth. Most space shuttles orbit at 200 to 240 miles above the earth.[32]

I don't believe we will need stairs, elevators, escalators, and the like to go from one level or area of the new Jerusalem to another. Do you? And we won't need to call out, "Beam me up, Scottie," to go from ground level to the top of the city, or anywhere in between. If the levels of the new Jerusalem were one mile cubed, there would be 1,500 levels in the city. While we don't know the city's layout, my point is there will be plenty of space for all of God's children, and so much to do there.

Also, consider that we haven't even focused on the new earth and its inhabitants. Am I sounding fanatical, excited, or what? As the gospel song says, "Just imagine heaven, what God's kingdom will be like."[33] I am convinced by God's word that we need to focus our spiritual eyes fully on heaven.

My brother in Christ, Bill Franklin, wrote a song that I've adopted over the years called "Space Flight." The lyrics fit appropriately here:

"SPACE FLIGHT"[34]

Verse I
I do not have a spacesuit, no equipment, and no gear,
But some day in one split second, I no longer will be here.
In the twinkling of an eyelash, I will leave for outer space,
Faster than the fastest rocket, propelled by the power of grace.

Refrain
Far beyond orbiting planets, I'll be weightless I'll be free,
When I reach those pearly portals, I'll not lose i-d-e-n-t-i-t-y.
I've signed up for a space flight. I've been training many years,
And there'll be no cancellation in the weather or the gear.

Verse II
All my senses will be quickened by a power never felt before,
Immortality shall hold me, Hallelujah ever-more.
Yes, I've signed up for a space flight, I've been training many years.
There'll be no cancellation, in the weather or the gear.

Verse III
Hallelujah, I am ready, When the trump sounds, I'll be gone,
There's a nail-scarred hand extended, I shall grasp it out beyond.
Hallelujah, I am ready, when the trump sounds, I'll be gone,
Hummm, hummm.

SIGHTS AND SOUNDS OF HEAVEN

Tag-Ending
Hallelujah, I am ready, when the trump sounds, I'll be gone,
There's a nail-scarred hand extended, I shall grasp it out beyond.

Words and music by Bill Franklin

As a side note, my father, Hubert Mayo "Buster" Kennett, has on his grave marker the following inscription, "Except a man's reach exceeds his grasp, what's a heaven for."[35] Our faith in God should exceed what we can tangibly grasp or it isn't faith. Why? Because "Now faith is the substance of things hoped for, the evidence of things not seen." (Hebrews 11:1). I'm confident that, one day soon, we will grasp Jesus' hand. For now, by faith, let us take His hand and, by the Holy Spirit's leadership, may we spiritually travel far beyond all this world can offer us: Because "(God) hath raised us up together, and made us sit together in heavenly places in Christ Jesus" (Ephesians 2:4–6).

My Dad passed away in 1974. One of his favorite country singers was Jim Reeves. Dad loved to hear him sing "Four Walls,"[36] and he enjoyed listening to the music of that song. Not long before his passing, he decided to write a song about all the Lord had done for us, and the words of that song follow:

"HE CONQUERED SIN"[37]

Verse I
Jesus, our blessed redeemer,
Sent from the Father on high.
Born of the virgin, Mary,
The paths of all men he tried.

continued

Refrain
He conquered sin,
Death, hell, and the grave.
He conquered sin,
My lost weary soul to save.

Verse II
They crowned him with thorns,
They nailed him to a tree.
They pierced him, they scourged him,
He died there for you and for me.

Verse III
They laid him in a tomb,
They thought they had conquered my Lord.
But he arose in all of His glory,
And ascended back to our God.

Words by Hubert Mayo Kennett

CHAPTER VII

SAN ANTONIO RIVER WALK, MILLION DOLLAR HIGHWAY, AND MAGNIFICENT MILE

38

Street of Pure Gold

> *"and the street of the city was pure gold,* as it were transparent glass..." (Revelation 21:21) (emphasis added).

San Antonio River Walk

My brother Jack A. Kennett and his wife Juanita live in the lovely community of Schertz, Texas, which is near San Antonio. I recall my first visit there in late 1995 while returning from a trip to Belize, Central America. Jack and Juanita took me on a tour of the San Antonio area, and highlights of our trip included visits to the Alamo and the famous "San Antonio River Walk," also known as the "Paseo del Rio." This river walk is a network of walkways along the San Antonio River, one story beneath San Antonio, Texas. Perhaps you have visited this beautiful area, as I have. But do you know its history?

A devastating flood occurred in the San Antonio area in 1921, which killed fifty people. That catastrophe led Robert Hugman, a San Antonio native and architect, to draft and submit plans that eventually brought about the first phase of the River Walk project in 1939. Since then the parallel sidewalks, connecting bridges, etc., have continued to expand. Today, hotels, shops, restaurants, and other establishments line the river walk areas. Two of San Antonio's most popular tourist attractions, the Alamo and "Paseo del Rio," are now connected via the River Walk.

By the way, a boat ride on the winding San Antonio River along the river walk is a must for tourists, and the River Walk's beautiful bald cypress trees, whose branches rise upward to as much as ten stories high, are a sight to behold. Other items of interest include the Hyatt Regency Hotel, which opened in 1981 with a pedestrian connector linking the Alamo Plaza with the river walk, waterfalls, waterways, and indigenous landscaping, and the recent opening of the $71.2 million dollar "Museum Reach of the River Walk."[39]

THE MILLION-DOLLAR HIGHWAY

In the state of Colorado, you can travel 105 miles on the U.S. 550 highway from Montrose to Durango through a section of the beautiful yet rugged, San Juan mountain range, known to the Ute Indians as the Shining Mountains. A unique part of this scenic drive is located between the towns of Silverton, a silver mining town, and Ouray. Ouray is a picturesque town nestled in a tiny bowl that is known as the "gem of the Rockies." This twenty-five mile stretch of US 550 was built during the 1930s, partly cut from the side of a mountain, and became known as the "Million Dollar Highway."

There are a variety of explanations regarding the origin of the name for this section of the highway. One version of the story claims it is based on the value of the ore-bearing fill used to construct the road, which some say included gold dust. Another says it refers to the high cost of building the road over the Red Mountain Pass (11,008 feet) and the Uncompahgre Gorge, which stretches approximately twelve miles. In any event, a million dollars was a fortune during that period, yet even considering today's cost estimates, the "Million Dollar Highway" cannot begin to compare to one mile of golden street in the new Jerusalem, as you will see.[40]

RONNIE S. KENNETT

The Magnificent Mile—
Chicago, Illinois

A dear friend, David Parker, who is president of the Extension Loan Fund, Inc., in Oklahoma City, Oklahoma (I served on that board for twelve years), told me about this area of Chicago, and although I have been through Chicago many times, I haven't toured the Magnificent Mile.

My research found that this area of North Michigan Avenue is one of the great avenues of the world. It is located in the heart of downtown Chicago and is an international tourism attraction. In addition, the Magnificent Mile is one of the most vibrant and successful commercial, residential, cultural, and tourist areas of the world.

The Magnificent Mile district includes thirteen blocks of North Michigan Avenue that runs from the banks of the Chicago River in the south and to Oak Street in the north, extending a full square mile from North Michigan Avenue. Also, it includes beautiful residences, premier retailers, trendy boutiques, distinctive restaurants, famous museums, luxurious hotels, landmark architecture, and prestigious educational and medical facilities.[41] In short, together with other beautiful and magnificent places throughout the earth that could be added to this chapter, there is no place on earth that will compare with the new Jerusalem.

One PowerPoint graphic that I use in teaching "Sights and Sounds of Heaven" relates to a hypothetical "what if": How much gold would it take to make one mile of golden street in this city of gold (the new Jerusalem), and what would the cost be using the U.S. gold standard?

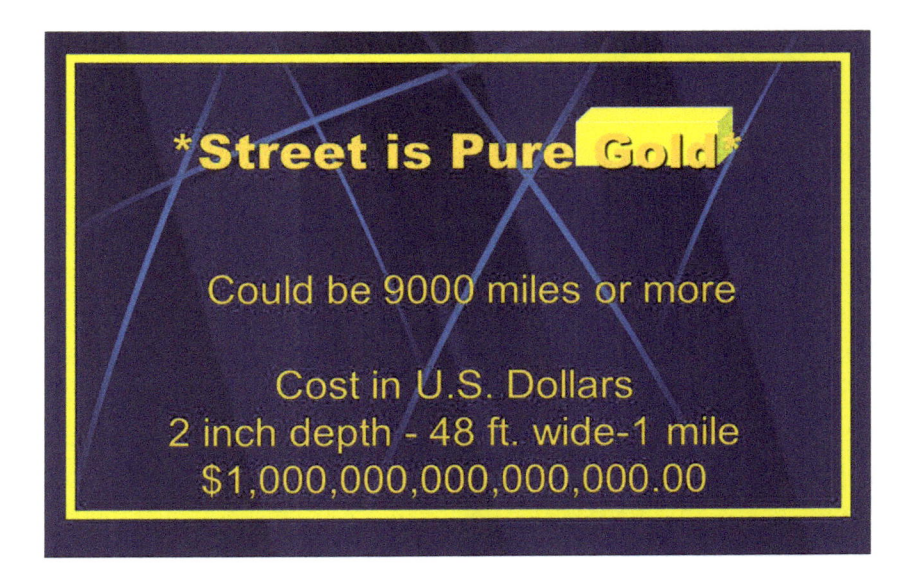

SIGHTS AND SOUNDS OF HEAVEN

> ***Street is Pure Gold***
>
> Could be 9000 miles or more
>
> Cost in U.S. Dollars
> 2 inch depth - 48 ft. wide-1 mile
> $1,000,000,000,000,000.00

More than fifteen years ago, I received a phone call from a close friend who happened to be a bank client as well. I told Floyd Giampocaro I needed his expertise and assistance in a personal matter, but it required him coming to my office. Floyd, who was an asphalt contractor, inquired further, so I informed him I needed to convert "asphalt to gold." I will never forget his response. "Ron, you're always up to something, but this takes the cake. I can't wait to see what you have in mind, so I'll see you shortly." After Floyd arrived, we proceeded to convert asphalt to gold. You see, I asked Floyd what tonnage of asphalt it would take to pave one mile of roadway, having a two-inch thickness and with a forty-eight-foot width. Floyd did his calculations and proceeded to give me the tonnage and then the current price. Next, Floyd asked me about the labor costs. I told him to "forget the labor." I informed him that no labor would be needed, since God had already placed streets of pure gold in the new Jerusalem and I wanted to develop a graphic using a "what if" example. I simply took the tonnage asphalt, and reduced tons to pounds and then to ounces. After that, I did my calculations based on the US price of gold at that time, which happened to be $360 a troy ounce. A street of pure gold one mile long, in US currency would have cost $315,000,000,000,000 (three hundred fifteen trillion dollars).

The above graphic reflects the current value of earthly gold, which at the time of this writing is approximately $1,300 per troy ounce and equates to $1,000,000,000,000,000.00 (rounded to one quadrillion dollars). Wow! Also, it is important to note that earth's gold isn't pure. The street in the new Jerusalem was made of pure gold as it were transparent glass (Revelation 21:21). And if the street begins at God's throne and ends at each entrance to the twelve gates, there could be 9,000 miles or more of golden streets on the first level! In my teachings, I often use this discussion to point out that our God is the only true and living God, and He is an awesome God.

My research led me to notice that many ethnologists believe there will be only one boulevard/highway in the new Jerusalem. Apparently, they reached their conclusions based on the fact that there is a street of gold, not streets of gold in the city. My comments above lead me to believe that if the new Jerusalem has twelve entrances, then God could surely have a street from each entrance leading to His throne, and I believe God has enough gold to connect the streets. After all, our earthly gold and silver will one day soon be cast into the streets (Ezekiel 7:19). Also, our earthly gold isn't pure gold. As a matter of fact, can we name anything on or in this earth that is pure other than a pure heart? I can't? Remember, Jesus Himself said during the beatitudes in His Sermon on the Mount: "Blessed are the pure in heart for they shall see God" (Matthew 5:8). And the only way any human being can be pure in heart is by accepting Jesus Christ as Savior and Lord and living a Christ-centered life.

SIGHTS AND SOUNDS OF HEAVEN

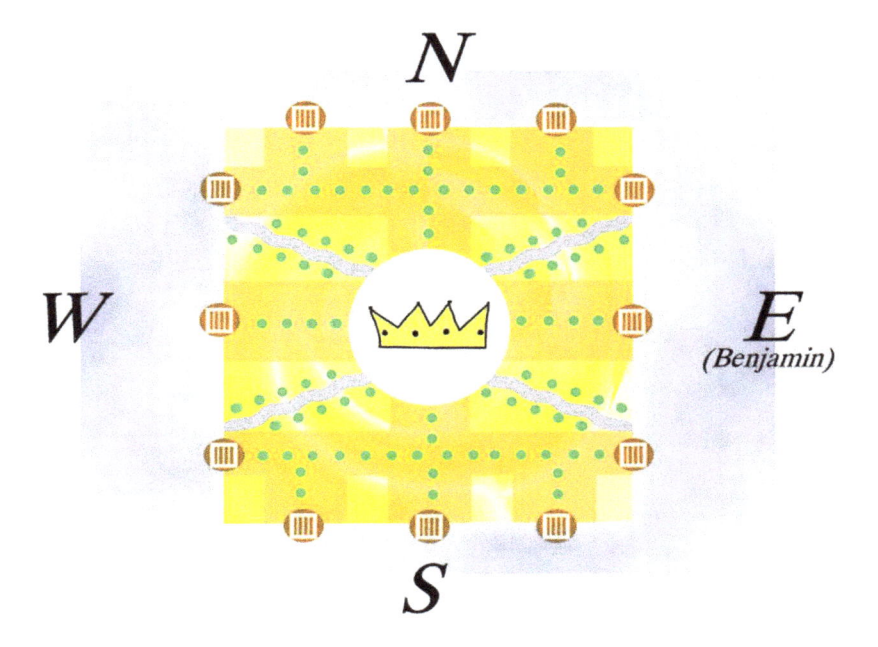

Revelation 22:1–2 tells us, "And he [the angel] shewed me a pure river of water of life, clear as crystal, proceeding out of the throne of God and of the Lamb. In the midst of the street of it, and on either side of the river, was there the tree of life, which bare twelve manner of fruits, and yielded her fruit every month: and the leaves of the tree were for the healing of the nations."

Continuing to focus on the golden street, we are told the tree of life is in the midst of the street and on both sides of the river. Therefore, we can reasonably consider two different scenarios. The river of life may flow down the center of the golden street with the tree(s) of life on either side of the river and in the midst of the street. Or, the river may flow from the throne in various directions, independent from the golden street, with the tree of life on either side of the river and in the midst of the street. I love this graphic, as it focuses on the center Eastern gate and illustrates the river of life flowing from the throne down the center of the street with tree(s) of life on either side of the river, yet in the midst of the street.

The previous graphic was designed to illustrate the river of life with tree(s) of life on either side, separated independently from the golden street and depicting scenario two. You will notice I have shown the name Benjamin at the center Eastern gate, as does Ezekiel 48:32. There is a specific reason for this, which I will explain in a later chapter. You may want to close your eyes and try to imagine the beauty of the golden street, river of life, and tree of life, all three intersecting with the throne of God and the Lamb. My wife, Rachel, and I were discussing the golden street, the tree of life, and the river of life. She commented that maybe God has placed at least twelve trees of life on each street and either side of the river of life, connecting to each gate and the throne. Hence, those who travel the street from the north, south, east, or west entrance gates will have access to the tree without having to travel in other directions. Regardless of the setting and because Scripture doesn't give us the exact locations of the throne, the street, or the river, it will be glorious and beautiful because Jesus will be there, and His beauty and glory will outshine everything else. What a city! Oh, what a Savior!

I'm sure there are many other places in the United States and throughout the world that provide similar spectacular scenic beauty and provide for equally enjoyable leisurely walks. However, no place on earth, for sightseeing, tourism, leisurely walks, or otherwise will compare with a walk on the new Jerusalem's golden street. After all, just as the city itself is transparent pure gold, so is the street of the city. I have stated many times that all of our earthly gold, which has impurities in it, cannot begin to compare with heaven's pure gold. On earth, we walk by faith, but in heaven faith will become reality, and we will stroll on street(s) of pure gold. My finite vocabulary can only think of one descriptive word here. Wow!

Before closing this chapter, I'm reminded of an incident that occurred during a presentation some years ago. I usually try to encourage audience participation, and at that time I requested the assistance of a dear minister friend who was attending the presentation for the first time. His name is Norman Arrington; he also performs powerful biblical monologues. I asked Norm to walk with me down glory avenue, past the tree(s) of life, turning onto hallelujah boulevard (my street names). As we walked, I reminded Norm to be careful not to bump into the tree of life and to be sure he turned at the intersection. I shall never forget his witty reply. Norm answered, "Ron, you'll need to guide me, for I haven't been here before." And, Norm, you were so right. We haven't seen the new Jerusalem yet, but when we arrive there, I would love to tour God's Pearly White City with you.

A Childhood "Boyish" Stroll

Let me take you back to former times when I was a young boy. You see, there's something to be said about the word "boy." I am the eldest of four sons born to Hubert Mayo and Elizabeth Uinda Kennett. The others, by birth, are Jackson Airwood (Jack), Frederick Eugene (Gene), and Hubert Michael (Mickey or Mike). Being the oldest, I tried to look after my younger brothers, and sometimes that wasn't easy. Every now and then, I must confess, I encountered some difficulties. Nothing too serious, mind you, but enough for Dad to get my attention. You see, when Dad called me Ronnie or son, I knew everything was all right. However, when Dad called me "Boy," I knew I was in t-r-o-u-b-l-e. You get the picture. Maybe you're starting to remember...Oh well, let's continue.

Dad played the guitar using a thumb pick and all fingers, similar to the Burl Ives style. He taught me to play by ear at eight or ten years of age. Many times, Dad and I would sing at home and at church, and as time passed Gene began singing with us. Jack had enlisted in the US Air Force, and Mike, being ten years younger than I, had not begun singing with us. After a while Dad developed considerable arthritis, and it became difficult for him at times. He had taught me many songs, especially hymns and ballads. One song still stands out above all the others. Dad and I (and later Dad, Gene, and I) would sing this song. Dad is in heaven now, and Gene, Mike, and I continue singing what I suppose you could call our signature song. It beautifully tells about the end of our earthly journey, when we reach our "beautiful heavenly home":

"WHEN I WALK UP THE STREETS OF HOME"[42]

Verse I
When my life here is past and the end comes at last,
I must cross o'er that dark rolling sea.
Cares forever will cease in that haven of peace,
There my soul shall forever be free.

Refrain
When I walk (walk, walk)
Up the (beautiful golden) streets,
Where the fair (fair, fair)
Angels (ever with rapture) roam.
I'll not count (count, count)
Time by (passing of days and) years
When I walk up the
Streets of (beautiful heavenly) home.

Verse II
In that Home of the Soul there are pleasures untold,
And the breezes of Love ever blow.
And perennial springs where the birds ever sing,
Not a sigh, not a care shall we know.

Verse III
Oh, how sweet it will be when we cross o'er that sea,
There to dwell in that fair heavenly land.
While the years roll along, we will sing Heaven's Song,
And live with the fair Angel Band.

Author unknown
(Public domain)

SECTION III

EARTHLY AND HEAVENLY PROPHETIC EVENTS

CHAPTER VIII

THE RAPTURE: "COME UP HITHER"

43

The apostle Paul was looking for Jesus Christ to return and rapture His church almost 2,000 years ago. Paul was the first to give us assurance in 1 Corinthians 15:52 that the rapture would occur "In a moment, in the twinkling of an eye, at the last trump: for the trumpet shall sound, and the dead shall be raised incorruptible, and we shall be changed." I have heard Jack Van Impe and others describe the "twinkling of an eye" to be eleven hundredths of a second. Wow! Words cannot describe our transformation from an earthly body to a heavenly body and our journey from earth to heaven.

We are reminded in 2 Corinthians 12:2–5 that Paul was caught up to the third heaven into paradise, and the Lord showed him many things that Paul was not allowed to convey to us in his epistles. I can only imagine the sights and sounds Paul must have seen and heard, but they must have been awesome, since he heard unspeakable words that are not lawful for a man to utter.

Perhaps Paul's description of the rapture here and in I Thessalonians 4:13–18 gives us a portion of all he saw and heard during his time in the third heaven. Of course, Jesus Himself promised when He returns to rapture His bride (Mathew chapter 24, Mark chapter 13, Luke chapter 21, and John chapter 14). And the two men (angels) who were present when Jesus ascended into heaven after His resurrection assured the disciples in Acts chapter 1:9–11 that "this same Jesus" will return in the same manner as you have seen Him go into heaven. This return will be to "catch away" His bride and is called the rapture.

In Revelation 4:1–11, John looked and saw a door opened in heaven. The first voice he heard sounded like a trumpet talking to him, and the voice said, "Come up hither, and I will shew thee things which must be hereafter." Then John sees a throne set in heaven, and He that sat on the throne was to look upon like a jasper (green/red) and a sardine (red) stone: and there was a "rainbow" round about the throne, in sight like unto an emerald (green). Let me remind you that the rainbow has seven colors that never change, beginning on the outer ring with red, next is orange, followed by yellow, after which is *green*: then comes blue, followed by indigo, and finally violet. I believe God's bow in this rainbow has the dominant color of green because green is the central color of the rainbow and represents life. I will discuss this further in another chapter. The bride of Christ will be in heaven with the Lord until the seventh year is finished, at which time the battle of Armageddon takes place as described in Revelation 19:11–21. Yes, we will return to earth with our Savior and Lord, Jesus Christ, riding white horses, and after Jesus Himself defeats the antichrist, the false prophet, and their armies and after the beast (antichrist) and false prophet are cast into the lake of fire, we will serve our precious Lord during the millennial reign here on earth.

44

CHAPTER IX

THE MARRIAGE SUPPER OF THE LAMB

> Blessed are they which are called to the marriage supper of the Lamb. (Revelation 19:9)

Revelation chapter 19:7–10 gives us some details regarding this subject, and many theologians have differing ideas as to exactly when, where, and for how long the "marriage supper" will take place. I have personally thought it will take place in heaven sometime during the seven-year tribulation (possibly the latter part).

In addition, I believe those who accept Jesus as Savior and die during this time will join those who were "caught up" in the rapture. It appears from Scripture that all Old Testament saints (Luke 13:29), as well as believers who will be martyred during the tribulation (Revelation 20:4), the redeemed of Israel, and believing gentiles saved during the great tribulation could join Christ for this marriage feast.

Just how long the marriage supper will last is not disclosed, and it may not last longer than the tribulation. However, many theologians believe it will occur just after the battle of Armageddon and/or during the millennial reign with Christ. Some hold that it will last the entire one thousand years. I do not adhere to that teaching and do not find it in God's Word.

While none of us know when and where our Lord will sit down with His wife at the marriage supper of the Lamb, I'm confident that everyone present will love sharing this supper with The King of kings and Lord of lords.

By God's grace I wouldn't miss it, and I pray you won't either.

CHAPTER X

THE SEVEN-YEAR GREAT TRIBULATION

Many theologians, ministers, and others have varying opinions as to just when the tribulation period will occur. I am pretribulation in my belief regarding the rapture. I also believe the antichrist and false prophet will come on the world scene soon after Jesus removes His bride from the earth. The beast (antichrist) will not only make war with the saints but will also be given power over all nations during this period of time (see Revelation 13:7–8) and will deceive many.

However, God will send two witnesses, primarily to turn people to Jesus Christ and also to bring judgments upon the earth. I believe these two witnesses will be Elijah and Moses; many believe the two will be Enoch and Elijah. It appears to me these witnesses will be on earth during the first three and a half years of the tribulation period, and after God allows them to be killed by the antichrist (Revelation 11:6–7), their bodies will lie in the streets of Jerusalem for three and a half days, after which they shall receive the Spirit of life from God and hear the same voice John heard saying "come up hither" (Revelation 4:1). Then these witnesses will ascend into heaven as fear grips those who watch this event all around the world (Revelation 11:11–12).

During this time the 144 thousand from the twelve tribes of the children of Israel are sealed (Revelation 7:4–8) and obviously will proclaim the gospel across the earth. They appear again singing a new song (Revelation 14:3).

There is so much that occurs during the seven-year tribulation period that I cannot pen here, but I felt the urgency to highlight some of them to encourage readers to recognize, as Jesus instructed John, that many things and events that have already happened, are happening, and will soon happen (Revelation1:19).

I remain convinced that the tribulation period is very near, and the walls of mankind are rapidly disintegrating. My mind goes back to the late 1980s when the Berlin wall was falling. During this time, I wrote this song in 1990:

"Man's Walls are Coming Down"[45]

Verse I
The story of the battle of Jericho in the Bible we recall,
Men thought they could defend themselves surrounded by a wall.
But God commanded Joshua seven days to march around,
Blow the trumpet and shout aloud and the wall will come down.

Refrain
Oh yes man's walls are coming down,
God's church is getting ready to leave the ground,
Just any day we'll hear His trumpet sound,
We'll meet Jesus in the air, go with Him to heaven fair,
Evermore we'll live up there for man's walls are coming down.

Verse II

Do you remember when they built the famous Berlin wall?
Some people said it was there to stay and it would never fall.
But God's performing miracles and His mercy still abounds.
So to set those people in bondage free,
Those walls had to come down.

Verse III

Religious walls have been built to satisfy some men,
Denying Jesus and His shed blood, He alone can save from sin.
God is telling His church today to stop our playing 'round,
For the Holy Ghost, in Jesus' name is bringing man's down.

Words and music by Ronnie S. Kennett

CHAPTER XI

THE SECOND COMING OF JESUS CHRIST AND THE BATTLE OF ARMAGEDDON

The rapture has taken place, the great tribulation is ending, and the second coming of our Savior and Lord, Jesus Christ, returning to earth riding a white horse with His bride and a heavenly host on white horses behind Him is the next event occurring. Wow! What a sight to behold!

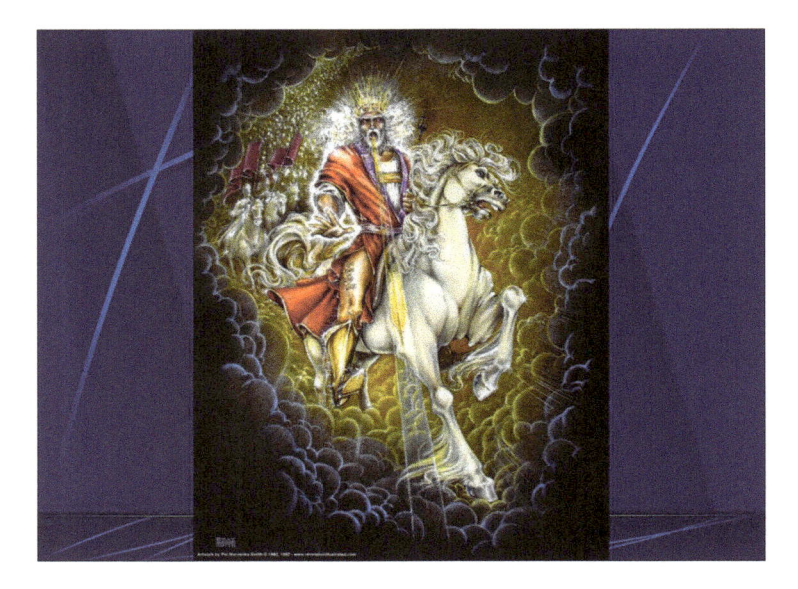

46

The antichrist, the false prophet, and his armies have gathered for war against the King of kings and His army. God's living Word (Jesus Christ), who is the Way, the Truth, and the Life, lets us know how quickly a battle can end (Revelation 19:20).

Jesus Christ fights this battle Himself and destroys the earthly armies as the heavenly armies of our Lord look on (see Revelation 19:21). No doubt these armies of heaven will include the bride of Christ, heavenly angels, and those who were beheaded during the great tribulation for refusing to take the mark of the beast and instead accepting Jesus as Savior and Lord. Jesus then has the antichrist and false prophet cast into the lake of fire (Revelation 19:20).

And then God sends an angel from heaven (I like to believe this angel will be the archangel Michael) who carries a key to the bottomless pit and a great chain. This angel lays hold of the dragon—the serpent Satan—and binds him for a thousand years. The angel casts Satan into the bottomless pit, places a seal on him so that he deceives the nations no more for the thousand years, and then he will be loosed for a season (Revelation 20:1–3).

When teaching *Sights and Sounds of Heaven*, I have often encouraged congregations to remember that our God is an *awesome* God. He sent only one angel to lay hold on Satan, bind him, cast him into the bottomless pit, shut him up, and set a seal upon him. My point is: God created Lucifer, and because he fell from heaven, God will take care of him as He has promised in Revelation 20:10.

CHAPTER XII

THE MILLENNIAL KINGDOM OF JESUS CHRIST

Jesus will rule with a rod of iron throughout the thousand years of His millennial reign (Revelation 19:15 and Psalm 2:7–9). He will probably begin this reign by judging the nations of earth at this time. Also, nation shall not lift sword against nation nor learn war anymore. During this time there will be no wars, and men will beat their swords into plowshares (Isaiah 2:4 and Micah 4:3). The feet of the King of kings and Lord of lords will stand upon the Mount of Olives, which is before Jerusalem on the east, and the Mount of Olives "shall be cleaved in the midst thereof toward the east and toward the west...and half of the mountain shall remove toward the north and half toward the south" (Zechariah 14:4).

Zechariah chapter 14 and especially verse 16 through verse 21 highlight and describe the millennial kingdom as Jesus rules from the throne of David for a thousand years. Yes, our Savior and Lord will bring about peace, joy, prosperity, long life, health, healing, the removal of sickness, and the birth of children during this time.

I should emphasize the fact that sin will not be eradicated during the millennium; however, Jesus will be in control. Also, there will be one language spoken during the millennium, and nobody will take God's name in vain.

After Satan is loosed for a season and goes out to deceive the nations Gog and Magog, to gather them to battle, this battle will be short-lived because fire will come down out of heaven and devour Satan's army, and the devil himself will be cast into the lake of fire, where the beast (antichrist) and false prophet are, and he shall be tormented day and night forever and ever (see Revelation 20:7–10). Praise the Lord!!

I now pause to remind you that the rapture of the bride, the second coming of our Lord Jesus Christ, and the millennial reign of Jesus have not occurred yet. However, I believe all of these events are near at hand.

I am reminded of a hymn written by James McPherson Kirk in 1894, which would be good to revive and include here:

"Our Lord's Return to Earth Again"[47]

Verse I
I am watching for the coming of that glad millennial day,
When our blessed Lord shall come and catch His waiting bride away.
Oh, my heart is filled with rapture as I labor, watch and pray,
For our Lord is coming back to earth again.

Refrain
Oh, our Lord is coming back to earth again,
Yes, our Lord is coming back to earth again.

*Satan will be bound a thousand years; we'll have no tempter then,
After Jesus shall come back to earth again.*

Verse II
Jesus' coming back will be the answer to earth's sorrowing cry,
For the knowledge of the Lord shall fill the earth and sea and sky.
God shall take away all sickness and the sufferer's tears will dry,
When our savior will come back to earth again.

Verse III
Yes, the ransomed of the Lord shall come to Zion then with joy,
And in all His holy mountain nothing hurts or shall destroy.
Perfect peace shall reign in every heart, and love without alloy,
After Jesus shall come back to earth again.

Verse IV
Then the sin and sorrow, pain and death of this dark world shall cease,
In a glorious reign with Jesus of a thousand years of peace.
All the earth is groaning, crying for that day of sweet release,
For our Jesus to come back to earth again.

Words and music by James M. Kirk

CHAPTER XIII

THE GREAT WHITE THRONE JUDGMENT

As sad as it is, the judgment mentioned in the caption must take place, and only those who are lost because they refused to accept Jesus Christ as Savior will be judged. Notice the word *white*, which symbolizes the absolute spotless holiness of God. Also, the word *great* certainly reflects God's authority, and He alone can bring judgment. We should always remember that God Elohim is triune (Father, Son, and Holy Spirit). Revelation 20:11 tells us that the heaven and the earth flee away from Him who sits on the great white throne, and there is found no place for them. We know that at some point after the millennium, God will create a new heaven and a new earth, and perhaps that creation change begins here.

In Revelation 20:11–15, all of the lost dead from all ages are raised from the dead and must appear at this judgment. Death and hell (hades) give up its dead, and the sea gives up its dead. The sea is mentioned specifically, since bodies in the oceans and seas will have been devoured into little bits and/or totally destroyed, yet God will see to it that these bodies will be resurrected so these individuals will stand before God's throne to be judged for their works.

Notice all will be judged fairly according to their works; however, those who failed to accept Jesus Christ as Savior and have sinned and come short of the glory of God are lost and thus are all condemned (Romans 3:23). We must remember that whosoever's name was/is not found written in the book of life will be cast into the lake of fire, which is the second death (Revelation 20:14–15). God has given us clear and concise information for our spiritual welfare. The lake of fire is a terrible doom, and Jesus paid the price on Calvary's cross to save us from our sins' penalty (John 3:16).

As you read the rest of *Sights and Sounds of Heaven*, if you haven't done so, read the eighteen words in Revelation 20:15. These words are very sobering. However, God has given each of us the opportunity to accept His Son Jesus Christ as Savior and Lord and live with Him in the new Jerusalem forever. The choice is ours, and my prayer is that you will become more excited than you have ever been as you spiritually see and hear the glories and splendors of heaven and the new Jerusalem that awaits us.

Revelation 20:11 reads, "And I saw a great white throne, and him that sat on it, from whose face the earth and the heaven fled away; and there was found no place for them." Compare this scripture with Revelation 21:1, "And I saw a new heaven and a new earth: for the first heaven and the first earth were passed away; and there was no more sea." These scriptures speak of the departing of the present earth and its atmospheric heavens in preparation of the new heaven and new earth. 2 Peter 3:10 further testifies to this: "But the day of the Lord will come as a thief in the night; in the which the heavens shall pass away with a great noise, and the elements shall melt with fervent heat, the earth also and the works that are therein shall be burned up." Keep in mind that the earthly taint of all sin and everything related to it will be burned up and forever done away with, and as John saw in Revelation 21:1, the first heaven and the first earth have been done away with. The new heaven and new earth now come in view.

SECTION IV

THE PEARLY WHITE CITY

CHAPTER XIV

THE WALL, ITS FOUNDATIONS, AND ITS GATES OF PEARL

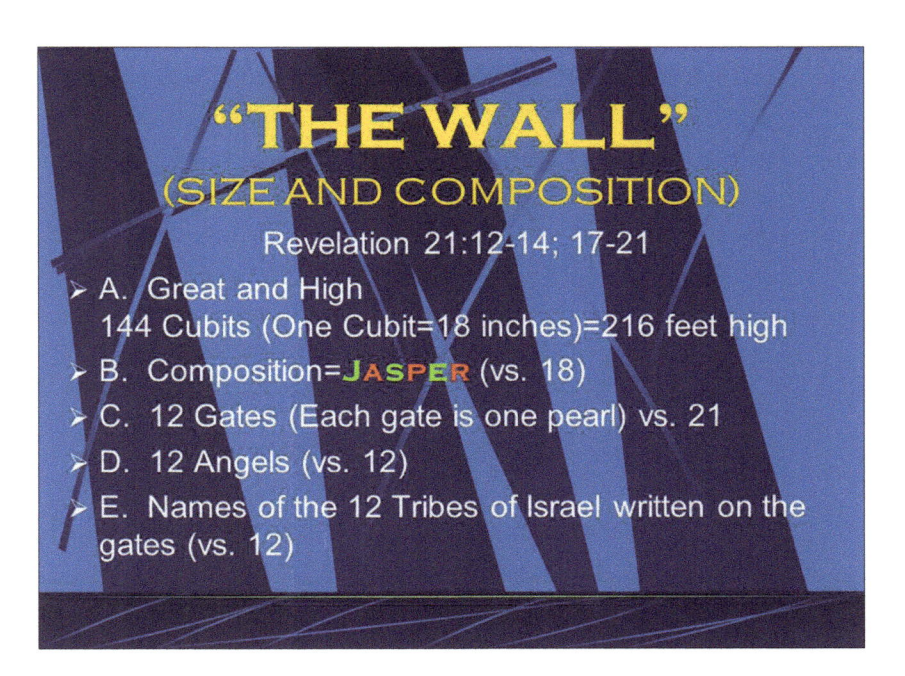

"THE WALL"
(SIZE AND COMPOSITION)
Revelation 21:12-14; 17-21
- A. Great and High
  144 Cubits (One Cubit=18 inches)=216 feet high
- B. Composition=**JASPER** (vs. 18)
- C. 12 Gates (Each gate is one pearl) vs. 21
- D. 12 Angels (vs. 12)
- E. Names of the 12 Tribes of Israel written on the gates (vs. 12)

SIZE OF CITY WALL

And [the city] had a wall great and high, and had twelve gates, and at the gates twelve angels, and names written thereon, which are the names of the twelve tribes of the children of Israel: on the east three gates; on the north three gates; on the south three gates; and on the west three gates. And the wall of the city had twelve foundations, and in them the names of the twelve apostles of the Lamb. And he that talked with me had a golden reed to measure the city, and the gates thereof, and the wall thereof. And the city lieth foursquare and the length is as large as the breadth: And he measured the city with the reed, twelve thousand furlongs. The length and the breadth and the height of it are equal.

And he measured the wall thereof, an hundred and forty and four cubits, according to the measure of a man, that is, of the angel. And the building of the wall of it was of *jasper*: And the city was pure gold, like unto clear glass. And the foundations of the wall of the city were garnished with all manner of precious stones. And the twelve gates were twelve pearls: every several gate was of one pearl: and the street of the city was pure gold as it were transparent glass.

(Revelation 21:12–21, emphasis added).

The first foundation was *jasper*; the second, sapphire; the third, a chalcedony; the fourth, an emerald; the fifth, sardonyx; the sixth, sardius; the seventh, chrysolyte; the eighth, beryl; the ninth, a topaz; the tenth, a chrysoprasus; the eleventh, a jacinth; the twelfth, an amethyst. And the twelve gates were twelve pearls; every several gate was of one pearl."

(Revelation 21:19b–21, emphasis added)

I consolidated the verses of Revelation 21 that pertain to the wall of the new Jerusalem, because there is so much to consider concerning the wall, including its gates and foundations. John gives us specific details concerning the new Jerusalem's wall, beginning with the fact that it is great and high. The angel measured it to be 144 cubits. A cubit is approximately 18 inches, which makes the wall 216 feet, either in height or width. We aren't told which; however, I believe this measurement relates to the height, while many theologians believe it is width. Regardless, it is great and high. The wall is composed of jasper. There are twelve gates in the wall, three each on the north, south, east, and west, with an angel (twelve in all) stationed at each gate.

The names of the twelve tribes of the children of Israel are engraved in the twelve gates. I believe these are the names of the twelve sons of Jacob and do not include either son of Joseph. There are twelve foundations of the wall and engraved therein are the names of the twelve apostles of the Lamb. Of course, these include eleven of the original twelve disciples, excluding Judas Iscariot, and the twelfth will be Matthias or Paul. I personally believe it will be the apostle Paul. Paul wrote thirteen New Testament books and possibly Hebrews. He begins nine of those books by letting the reader know he was an apostle called of God and our Lord, Jesus Christ. I firmly believe his name will be in one of the twelve foundations, and you will notice that I have named Paul first on the graphic listing the twelve apostles in the twelve foundations in my selected order.

We are not given the exact order for the twelve tribes or the twelve apostles. The twelve foundations will be garnished with the twelve precious stones referenced earlier, and I will specifically discuss those in chapter XV and XVI.

Great Wall of China

I haven't been to the Great Wall of China, but I have heard much about it and read about it. I'm told that more than a million tourists visit it annually. One of the great wonders of our world, this wall winds approximately 4,163 miles from east to west in China and has a history of over 2,300 years. I read that one man walked the entire length of the wall, and it took him over two years to complete the trek.[48] I suppose that wall must be a sight to behold. However, I can assure you nothing on earth, including China's Great Wall, will even remotely compare with the new Jerusalem's wall, which encompasses the entire city. This means the length of the wall could be approximately 9,000 miles or more than twice the length of China's wall.

When we look closely at the aforementioned descriptions and glimpses, we see they are only the beginnings of all that await God's children when we finally get "Home." I am so happy that we will have a new body, because there will be so much to tour and view, just of the new Jerusalem's wall. Imagine the beauty of this massive wall made of jasper. My research leads me to believe it is brilliant translucent green in color with red spots in it. I will have more detailed comments regarding jasper later. So, why don't we take a brief tour of the wall. Before we do, please review the following graphic.

SIGHTS AND SOUNDS OF HEAVEN

NAMES ON THE 12 GATES OF THE WALL
12 TRIBES OF THE CHILDREN OF ISRAEL
(vs. 12)
JACOB'S SONS (GENESIS 29, 30, 35)

Name	Mother
1. REUBEN	LEAH
2. SIMEON	LEAH
3. LEVI	LEAH
4. JUDAH	LEAH
5. DAN	BILHAH (RACHEL'S HANDMAID)
6. NAPHTALI	BILHAH (RACHEL'S HANDMAID)
7. GAD	ZILPAH (LEAH'S HANDMAID)
8. ASHER	ZILPAH (LEAH'S HANDMAID)
9. ISSACHER	LEAH
10. ZEBULAN	LEAH
11. JOSEPH	RACHEL
12. BENJAMIN	RACHEL

THE GATES OF THE NEW JERUSALEM

Having already briefly described components of the wall, let us consider and view in greater detail the twelve gates located in the wall. According to Revelation 21:13, there are twelve gates in the wall, and each gate is one pearl. Three gates of pearl are on the east, north, south, and west sides of the wall with one angel stationed at each gate.

The names of the twelve sons of Jacob are written thereon (at each gate); and, according to birth, are Reuben, Simeon, Levi, Judah, Dan, Napthali, Gad, Asher, Issacher, Zebulan, Joseph, and Benjamin. Their names could be engraved in the gates exactly as Ezekiel identifies them in Ezekiel 48:30–34. Thus, the number twelve, which means government, leaps out as we behold twelve gates, twelve angels, and twelve names related to this area alone.

Gates of Pearl

Can you imagine beholding and walking in and out of those beautiful gates of *pearl*? I try to visualize each gate of pearl as an enormous white orb. I suppose that is why we can call the new Jerusalem "the pearly white city." When I'm teaching about heaven, I enjoy comparing the pearls a lady wears to these gates made of pearl. My usual comment is, "No oyster has ever produced a pearl to compare with the beauty, size, and splendor of these beautiful 'pearly gates.'" Surely, we will need our immortal eyes in heaven, since these earthly eyes could not see what my feeble words are trying to describe to you. With the walls of the new Jerusalem being 216 feet high (or thick), we can only imagine the size of each gate of pearl.

SIGHTS AND SOUNDS OF HEAVEN

THE PEARL OF GREAT PRICE

Don Harris has been a jeweler in Bluefield, Virginia, for more than forty years. During my research regarding pearls and especially this book section, my brother Mike and I had lunch with Don. We discussed various types of gems, specifically the new Jerusalem's twelve foundation stones and the twelve stones on the high priest's breastplate. Don commented that while precious stones are beautiful, the brilliance and *purity* of an untainted pearl have always intrigued him.

Further discussion led to the fact that Bible students can't talk about pearls without referring to Matthew 13:45–46, where Jesus talks about "the pearl of great price." Of course, this pearl is Jesus Christ. He alone is the only human being who was conceived by the Holy Spirit, born of the Virgin Mary, and lived a sinless, pure, holy life on this earth. No one else was found worthy to bear our sins in His own body and die on that "old rugged cross," freely paying the penalty God required to cleanse from all sin whosoever receives Him as Savior and Lord. Yes, Jesus, the "Pearl of Great Price," died, was buried, rose again the third day, and showed Himself to more than 500 witnesses during the following forty days. Then He ascended into heaven and is now seated at the right hand of God our Father, making intercession for you and me, conditioned only on our asking Him and believing by faith.

Nacre, also known as "mother of pearl," is an organic-inorganic composite material produced by some mollusks as an inner shell layer. It is strong, resilient, and iridescent. The nacre substance is called "mother of pearl" because it is the mother of true pearls. The ideal pearl is perfectly round and smooth. Interesting as well is the fact that *iridescent* comes from the Greek word *iris*, which means "rainbow." Thus, pearls can reflect hues of various colors, as do other precious stones.[50] It is likely that the gates of pearl may reflect hues other than white, as we will see later when we discuss other facts showing how much God loves colors.

Just as a beautiful untainted pearl is pure and free from imperfections, Jesus cleanses, purifies, and declares His children pure, unspotted, and worthy to become His church and His bride. He will clothe us with clean, spotless, and white garments, which is the righteousness of His saints (Revelation 19:8). Only by willingly choosing to receive His blood's cleansing power can we enter in and go in and out through the "pearly gates" of the new Jerusalem (Revelation 21:27 and 22:14). Why? Because, just as those beautiful white pearl orbs will be pure, all who pass through those gates must be pure as well. The words of an old hymn tell us, "Heaven is a holy place filled with glory and with grace, and sin can never enter there."[51]

The Foundations of the Wall

As I previously stated, the foundations of the wall are garnished with twelve precious stones. The first foundation is *jasper*; the second, sapphire; the third, chalcedony; the fourth, emerald; the fifth, sardonyx; the sixth, sardius; the seventh, chrysolite; the eighth, beryl; the ninth, topaz; the tenth, chrysoprasus; the eleventh, jacinth; and the twelfth, amethyst (Revelation 21:19–20).

Hebrews 11:10 tells us that Abraham "looked for a city which hath foundations, whose builder and maker is God." This scripture has always intrigued me for the following reasons. After John beholds the new heaven and new earth, he sees the new Jerusalem coming down from God, out of heaven, prepared as a bride adorned for her husband (Revelation 21:2). Then, the angel carries John to a high mountain to show him the bride, the Lamb's wife, where John beholds the city again "[h]aving the glory of God: and her light was like unto a stone most precious, even like a *jasper* stone, clear as crystal" (Revelation 21:11, emphasis added). If the new Jerusalem, as John sees it, is suspended above the new earth, and I believe it is, why did God use twelve foundations in the wall? I think the new Jerusalem will set suspended above the earth because John views it from a great and high mountain, and the nations of the earth shall walk in the light of the city (Revelation 21:24).

I have read and heard that many theologians believe there will be day and night on the new earth. I don't think so. Everyone who lives in the new Jerusalem and on the new earth will be saved, redeemed, pure, righteous, and holy children of God, and even the kings of the new earth will bring the glory and honor of the nations into the city. (See Revelation 21:24–27.) The gates will forever be open, and since there will be no night there, I believe the radiant beams of God's *Son-light* will shine brightly throughout the new Jerusalem and the new earth in that eternal *day*.

I have always considered Abraham's prophecy concerning the foundations (Hebrews 11:8–10) as pointing us to the joining of Israel (the twelve tribes on the gates) and the church/bride (twelve apostles on the foundations), in heaven/the new Jerusalem (Revelation 21:14). After all, Jesus promised that we will sit down with Abraham, Isaac, and Jacob, and He promised the apostles that they would join Him in His kingdom.

NAMES IN THE TWELVE FOUNDATIONS
TWELVE APOSTLES OF THE LAMB (VS. 14)

Name	Spiritual Attributes
1. Paul	Salvation
2. Peter	Faith
3. Andrew	Strength
4. James	Wisdom
5. John	Love
6. Phillip	Power
7. Bartholomew (Nathaniel)	Imagination
8. Matthew	Will
9. Thomas	Understanding
10. James (Son of Alpheus)	Order (Law)
11. Simon Zelotes	Zeal
12. Judas (Jude)	Renunciation

I have listed the names and order of the twelve apostles who I believe will be in the twelve foundations of the wall. They are Paul, Peter, Andrew, James, John, Phillip, Bartholomew (or Nathaniel), Matthew, Thomas, James (son of Alpheus), Simon Zelotes, and Judas (also called Jude). The apostles' names may not be in exact order, and it is certainly possible Matthias will be included instead of Paul. However, Acts 1:25–26 states that Matthias was appointed to "take part of this ministry and apostleship....and he was numbered with the eleven apostles."

However, I remain convinced that Paul will be listed with the twelve apostles. Let me recite the reasons why I believe Paul will be listed with the other apostles. First, I commented earlier that Paul wrote at least thirteen New Testament books, and in the opening chapters of nine of these books he named himself as "an apostle," called by God and Jesus. I am fully aware that Paul doesn't count himself worthy of apostleship, but God has called and sent many who didn't deem themselves worthy. Second, Paul speaks about heaven more than all the other New Testament writers, except possibly John (primarily in Revelation). Third, Paul was the only person recorded in the New Testament, other than John, who was "caught up to the third heaven...into paradise, and heard unspeakable words" (2 Corinthians 12:2–5). He wrote to the Philippians, "For me to live is Christ, and to die is gain.... For I am in a strait betwixt two, having a desire to depart, and to be with Christ; which is far better" (Philippians 1:21–24).

Paul's words to Timothy in 2 Timothy 4:6–8 are surely some of the most powerful words in Scripture by a child of God who knew they were soon departing this earth to be with Christ. He was ready to go; his departure was at hand; he had fought a good fight and finished his course; and he had kept the faith. May we, as Paul did, look for the soon return of our Lord Jesus Christ, assured that our destination is heaven.

Revelation 22:14 states, "Blessed are they that do his commandments, that they may have right to the tree of life, and may enter in through the gates into the city [new Jerusalem]." Revelation 22:17 states, "And the Spirit and the bride say, Come. And let him that heareth say, Come. And let him that is athirst come. And whosoever will, let him take of the water of life freely." Notice the tree of life and water of life are both in the new Jerusalem; therefore, all who do His commandments and are athirst (the redeemed) will have access to the new Jerusalem.

CHAPTER XV

THE TWELVE PRECIOUS GEMSTONES

Twelve Precious Stones

I realize I have written, to some degree earlier in this book, concerning these precious stones, which are in the twelve foundations of the wall. However, I am compelled to devote this chapter completely to them, because I believe they are significant in tying Israel and the bride together in the new Jerusalem. Some questions that I have encountered over the years relate to jasper and include the following:

- Why is the wall jasper?
- Why is the first foundation in the wall jasper?
- Why is the light of the city a jasper light?
- Why is jasper the twelfth precious stone in the high priest's breastplate, in Exodus chapter 28?
- Why, in Revelation 4:3, is "he that sat (on the throne) was to look upon like a jasper and a sardine stone"?

These questions about jasper led me to much prayer and research. I trust that you will see what I have discovered in prayerfully studying and researching these precious stones.

RONNIE S. KENNETT

TWELVE FOUNDATIONS OF THE WALL (vs. 19-20)

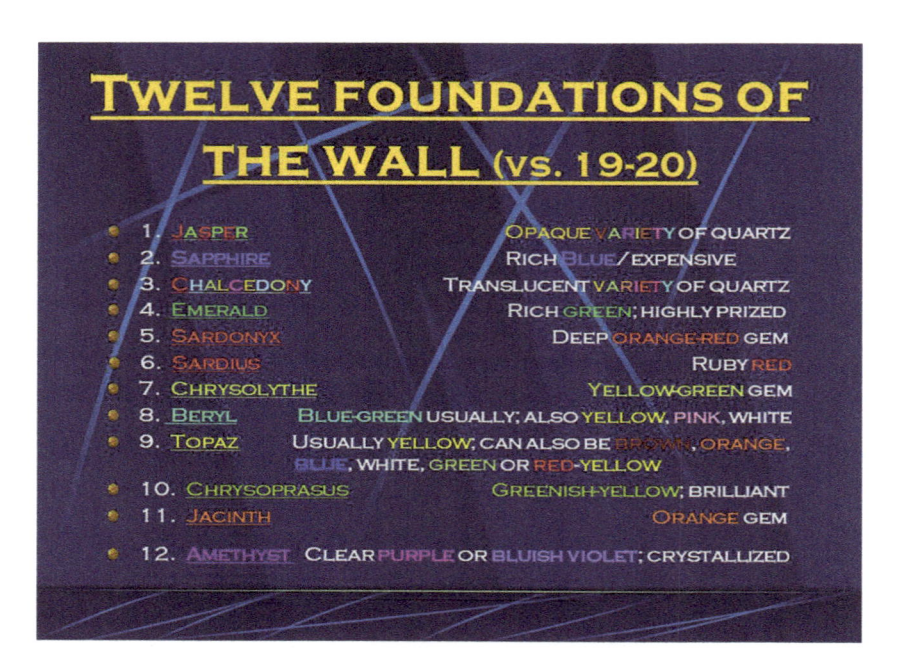

1.	JASPER	OPAQUE VARIETY OF QUARTZ
2.	SAPPHIRE	RICH BLUE / EXPENSIVE
3.	CHALCEDONY	TRANSLUCENT VARIETY OF QUARTZ
4.	EMERALD	RICH GREEN; HIGHLY PRIZED
5.	SARDONYX	DEEP ORANGE-RED GEM
6.	SARDIUS	RUBY RED
7.	CHRYSOLYTHE	YELLOW-GREEN GEM
8.	BERYL	BLUE-GREEN USUALLY; ALSO YELLOW, PINK, WHITE
9.	TOPAZ	USUALLY YELLOW; CAN ALSO BE BROWN, ORANGE, BLUE, WHITE, GREEN OR RED-YELLOW
10.	CHRYSOPRASUS	GREENISH-YELLOW; BRILLIANT
11.	JACINTH	ORANGE GEM
12.	AMETHYST	CLEAR PURPLE OR BLUISH VIOLET; CRYSTALLIZED

THE FOUNDATIONS' COLORS

The graphic titled "Twelve Foundations of the Wall" illustrates my research conclusions relative to the composition(s) and probable color(s) of these precious stones. I am well aware that we cannot begin to comprehend the beauty we shall behold when we see the wall of jasper and twelve foundations, with the brilliance of the colors of the rainbow, probably in varieties of hues we can't begin to imagine. I'm reminded of the new LCD and LED television sets advertising the millions of breathtaking colors we can view. Of course, the manufacturers want to sell their new products by convincing us of how vivid the colors will be, with beautiful scenery, animals, skin tones, etc. Commercials and store displays show vivid, beautiful pictures that look and seem "out of this world." Perhaps we should pause for a moment and thank our Savior and Lord for preparing an eternal city of pure gold, where *all things* are made *new*, with breathtaking color(s), beauty, and splendor that our finite minds cannot imagine and that will really be "out of this world."

My mind goes back to a particular night years ago (the 1970s to be more exact). While traveling home from a revival service where God had blessed gloriously, I was impressed by the Holy Spirit to stop by the roadside and pen the words to a song. I titled the song "Heaven By and By." At that time, I had no idea that I would be teaching about heaven and now writing this book. The song goes like this:

"Heaven By and By"[53]

Verse I
There's a place where the street is purest gold,
Of its beauty, oh, the half can ne'er be told.
Where there cometh no night, for Jesus is the light,
In heaven, sweet heaven, by and by.

Refrain
Don't you want to go to heaven,
Sweet heaven, by and by,
To live with Jesus, up there, no more to die.
On heaven's golden shore,
We'll sing His praise forevermore,
In heaven, sweet heaven, by and by.

Verse II
Oh, dear friend, do you have a sin-sick heart,
Knowing not which way to go, or where to start?
Let Jesus save you from your sin,
He'll give you peace and joy within,
He'll take you to heaven, sweet heaven, by and by.

Words and music by Ronnie S. Kennett

May I remind you that although my finite words cannot give you more than a glimpse of heaven, we can rest assured that our immortal eyes will view its splendor and beauty in "living color," which will be glorious and "worth all of our struggles in this earthly life."

As you examine the variety of colors in the twelve foundations/precious stones graphic, you may notice two things that are obvious. First, there is one color that stands out more than all others. Do you see it? Question #1, which follows, gives the answer and my reasoning. Second, there is a color that isn't shown in this graphic. Why isn't that color included? Question #2 details my answer and research regarding this color. This is only my opinion based on my research and is not meant to diminish any color or to add to or take away from God's precious Word. I understand how sensitive many people are today regarding color, most especially skin color. However, I believe it is important for me to convey what I have researched, studied, and taught as part of *Sights and Sounds*. I always ask and try to adequately answer these questions.

Question #1: Does God Have a Favorite Color, and If So, What Is It?

The Bible, the variety of colors throughout the earth, and the rainbow all provide evidence that God loves color. We know a rainbow is composed of the entire spectrum of colors of visible light, from the longest wavelength, red, to the shortest wavelength, violet. The order of the seven colors in a rainbow is easily remembered by the mnemonic formula ROY G. BIV: R=red, O=orange, Y= yellow, G=green, B=blue, I=indigo and V=violet. Red is at the top edge of the rainbow, and violet is at the bottom edge with the other colors in between.[54] Let me add that God set the rainbow in the sky to tell Noah (and us) that He will never destroy the earth again by a flood of water. He orchestrated the specific color spectrum with a specific number of colors that never change, and He called the rainbow "My Bow" (Genesis 9:12–17). Morris Cerullo is right: God has His perfect plan, purpose, design, and objectivity.[55]

Recognizing that God loves and made all colors, if He has a favorite color, I believe it is *green*. Did you notice that green is the central color of the rainbow? Maybe God designed green to be the center color of the rainbow to emphasize life and to illuminate the other six colors. As my dear friend and mentor Colonel Jack Kelley used to tell me when he wanted to get his point across, "Just a thought."

I continually ask people what color on earth they see more than any other. The answer, most often, is green. Green grass, green leaves on trees, green shrubs, and green plants. Yes, green, green, and greener.

Green depicts life as well. Chlorophyll is the green pigment found in tree leaves, plants, and marine algae; and through photosynthesis chlorophyll is "the blood of plants," transforming carbon dioxide into oxygen and thus life. Scientists tell us that chlorophyll is green, and green is life. While I am certainly not a scientist, my research found that the Greek definition for *chlorophyll* is green, and further, that chlorophyll is only one molecule away from hemin (hemoglobin), which is the red constituent of blood.[56] This led me to my reason for thinking God's favorite color is green. You may not agree with me...I haven't convinced my wife yet, either. Her favorite color is red. What is yours: blue, yellow, violet, etc.? My point is to inform you that all color hues are beautiful, and I'm confident heaven will fully exhibit various color schemes that only our immortal eyes can comprehend.

I recall presenting "Sights and Sounds" in a church where good friends and relatives, Jimmy and Connie Black, were the pastors. I'll never forget Connie's response when I suggested that God's favorite color might be green. She said, "I think I'll change my last name from Black to Green."

Question #2: Is There One Color That May Not Be Present in the New Jerusalem?

In attempting to answer this question, I am well aware of the sensitivity of the word *color* and the word *race* in our world today and especially in America. I was born in 1938 and grew up in the small coal-mining town of McComas, West Virginia. Our community was a melting pot of different nationalities: American, African American, Irish, Hungarian, and Italian. While the different nationalities lived in a coal camp community together, we knew one another, worked together, played together, attended school and church together, etc. I highlight this to tell you I didn't know that problems related to ethnicity, race, etc., existed until Rachel and I married and moved to other locations.

You will notice, the color black is not shown in any of my precious stone color descriptions. Why not? In conducting my research regarding the variety of colors in the twelve precious stones, I did not find black as a color of any specific stone. God has further demonstrated this by the pigmentation of human skin, the sky, earth, birds, food and plant life, etc. God made His human family in a diversity of colors, ranging from white hues to brown hues to red and yellow hues, etc., as I will attempt to clarify next.

When I am teaching on heaven, I always wear a white shirt. My purpose in doing so is to emphasize the color of my skin, when compared to my white shirt. By definition, in today's society, I am of the white race or Caucasian. However, when I ask congregations to compare the color of my skin to my white shirt, they always laugh. Apparently, my skin color isn't white at all (I sure don't think so).

I have been privileged to share this teaching in congregations or groups made up of peoples from various cultural, ethnic, and religious backgrounds. Several years ago, I presented it to five different congregations at a church in Harrisonburg, Virginia. There were white, black, Hispanic, and mixed congregations together for this service. I had already done extensive research regarding the color black prior to this service, and I was anxious to present some interesting facts I had discovered. My interests in such research centered on the fact that the rainbow colors do not include black, nor, in my opinion, do any of the precious stone colors. I questioned myself as to why I hadn't noticed the color black in any of the precious stones in the wall and foundation descriptions.

I have a black onyx ring and understand many of our earthly precious stones either are black or contain black in them. However, my research and studies have not found the color black as a component of any of the precious stones in the wall or foundations. Further inquiries led me to discover a variety of definitions for the word *black*, especially its skin-color definition when compared to its other definitions, and this requires further explanation.

When I am speaking or writing, I clearly define *black*, or African American peoples, as those people who have primarily dark to light brown pigmentation of skin and/or those whose skin pigmentation contains the color black.

The human family is made in God's image, after His likeness (Genesis 1:26–27). Even science has confirmed that there are absolutely minimal differences in the nationalities or races that are part of the human family except for our various skin colors created by skin pigmentation.[57] I use the words "human family" to emphasize the fact that all kindred, tongues, and nations of this earth have descended from Adam and Eve, which makes us one family. Although God confused man's languages and caused man's dispersion throughout the world, beginning at the Tower of Babel (see Genesis 11:1–9), man has created the "race" word and the differentiation of peoples on earth.

Perhaps I may burst some bubbles, but may I emphasize that God will have only His family in heaven. I don't believe there will be races and various families there, although there may be various skin colors. I haven't found an answer to this question in Scripture, except in 1 Corinthians 13:12, which says: "For now we look through a glass darkly, but then face to face: now we know in part; but then I know as even I am known." Also, we are all God's children. Let me add here as has often been said, "God doesn't have any grandchildren."

We don't know if the pigmentation to create various skin colors will be included as a part of God's heavenly family or not. We do know that we will have a new body "fashioned like unto his glorious body" (Philippians 3:21). John described Jesus in Revelation 1:14–15: "His head and his hairs were white like wool, as white as snow; and his eyes were as a flame of fire; and his feet like unto fine brass, as if they burned in a furnace; and his voice as the sound of many waters." The wonderful facts are we shall be like Him, we shall be with Him, we shall be worshipping Him, and we shall be praising Him forever! What a glorious thought!

Regarding God's rainbow of colors, it appears to me there will be no black in the new Jerusalem, unless we retain our earthly skin colors. The reason that black, in any other form, won't be in the new Jerusalem is that one distinct definition for *black* is: "the darkest color, devoid of light, completely dark, the color of coal or carbon, sin, evil, outer darkness, badness, etc."[58] We know that sin can never enter heaven, in any form, and there will be no darkness or night there. Heaven will be one eternal day, for His light dispels all darkness. Personally, I don't believe there will even be a shadow there. James 1:17 tells us, "Every good gift and every perfect gift is from above, and cometh down from the Father of lights, with whom is no variableness, neither shadow of turning." And, Revelation 21:23–25 clearly points us to the new light both of the new Jerusalem and the nations of the earth:

> And the city had no light of the sun, neither of the moon, to shine in it: for the glory of God did lighten it, and the Lamb is the light thereof. And the nations of them which are saved shall walk in the light of it: and the kings of the earth do bring their glory and honour in to it. And the gates of it shall not be shut at all by day: for there shall be no night there.

CHAPTER XVI

HIGH PRIEST BREASTPLATE/ PRECIOUS GEMSTONES (OLD TESTAMENT) COMPARED TO NEW JERUSALEM'S PRECIOUS GEMSTONES

I heard George Younce of the Cathedral Quartet recite the following poem or song, which, I think, fits perfectly with this question and answers portions of this color section of *Sights and Sounds*:

"How Beautiful Heaven Must Be"[59]

Verse I
If I had all the words in our language to use at a
moment's command,
If I had all the beautiful pictures of nature, the sea, and the land.
If I spoke in a voice never-ending; speaking only of loveliness,
I couldn't begin to tell you how beautiful heaven is.

continued

Verse II
If I mixed all the glorious sunsets with fathomless
mysteries of Mars,
If I mixed all the beauty of springtime: with the gleam of the
moon and the stars.
If I added the love of all mothers and the thrill of a baby's kiss,
I couldn't begin to tell you how beautiful heaven is.

Verse III
If I had all the hues of the rainbow translated into
beautiful words,
If I had all the magical music and if I had all the songs of
the birds,
If I had all the wisdom of sages to help me my themes express,
No, I couldn't begin to tell you how beautiful heaven is.

Verse IV
I never, no never could tell you how beautiful heaven is
I never, no never could envision its magical loveliness,
If the gift of the silvery-haired masters and prophets I
could possess,
I couldn't, no I really couldn't begin to tell you how beautiful
heaven is.

Song written by Mrs. A.S. Bridgewater,
music by A.P. Bland,
poem by George Younce
(public domain)

I have mentioned the twelve gates and the names of the twelve tribes of the children of Israel. Now, let us compare the twelve precious stones in the wall's foundations with the twelve precious stones in the high priest's breastplate, as found in Exodus chapter 28. Since the Old Testament was written primarily in Hebrew and the New Testament was written in Greek, some of the names of the precious stones in the breastplate differ from the names of the precious stones in the foundations. The names of seven precious stones are identical. Those stones are sardius, topaz, emerald, sapphire, amethyst, beryl and *jasper*. The names of five of the precious stones are different, but, from my research, I have concluded that the precious stones in the breastplate and in the foundations are all the same, as shown in the graphic. Listed below are the five stones in the high priest's breastplate that have names different from those in the twelve foundations of the wall, together with my conclusions regarding the foundation names and number found in Revelation 21:19–20.

Breastplate Stone	Foundation Stone	Foundation Number
Carbuncle	Sardonyx	Five
Diamond	Chrysolythe	Six
Ligure	Jacinth	Seven
Agate	Chalcedony	Eight
Onyx	Chrysoprasus	Eleven

While some people may differ with my analysis, I remain comfortable with my graphic comparisons. I always wear a replica of the high priest's breastplate while discussing this graphic (see above) and comparing it with the twelve precious stones in the twelve foundations graphic.

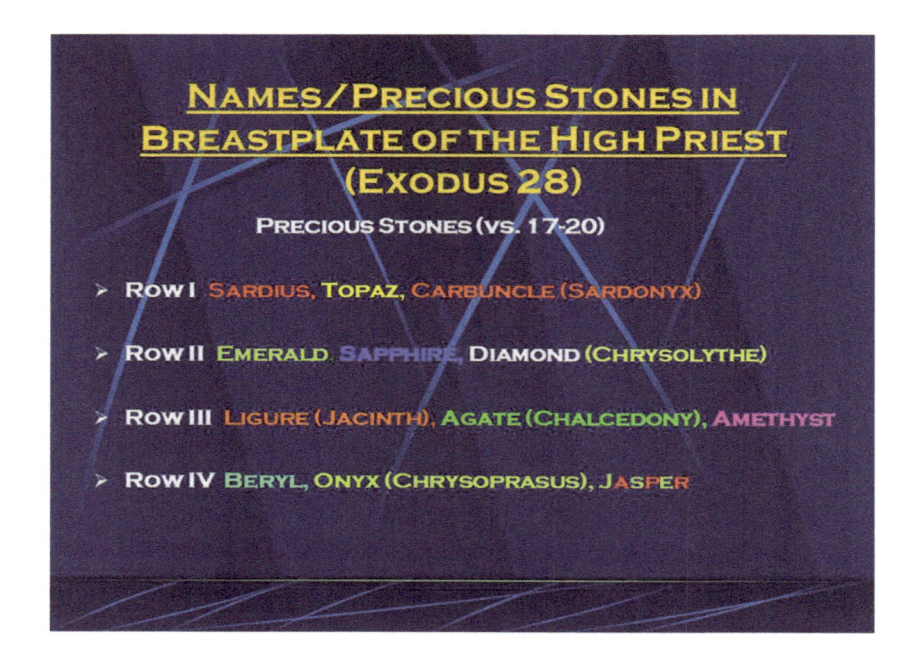

Names/Precious Stones in Breastplate of the High Priest (Exodus 28)

Precious Stones (vs. 17-20)

- Row I Sardius, Topaz, Carbuncle (Sardonyx)
- Row II Emerald, Sapphire, Diamond (Chrysolythe)
- Row III Ligure (Jacinth), Agate (Chalcedony), Amethyst
- Row IV Beryl, Onyx (Chrysoprasus), Jasper

CHAPTER XVII

THE PRECIOUS GEMSTONE JASPER

While doing my research and analysis of the twelve precious stones, I became more inquisitive about the jasper stone, which represents Jacob's son Benjamin and is the twelfth precious stone in the high priest's breastplate. I'm confident that every color of the rainbow, and their various hues, will be beautiful to behold. I also believe that jasper will shine brilliantly as the wall's radiance, as well as the first foundation, the light of the new Jerusalem and especially as He (Jesus) sits on the throne, in Revelation 4:3.

For two years I asked the Lord why the first foundation, the wall, and the light of the new Jerusalem, as well as He who sat on the throne in Revelation 4: 3 and Benjamin's stone in the high priest's breastplate are all *jasper*. One day after "I had a bad day at the office," I left a board meeting, returned to my office, and sat down, with my head in my hands, to have my pity party. Suddenly, I heard a voice saying, "You will find the answer to jasper in the lobby of this bank." I remember looking around the office, saw no one, disregarded the voice, and went back to my pity party. I heard the voice again, repeating the same words, and sensing the Holy Spirit speaking to me, I went to the office doorway and surveyed the lobby area. I confess, I was puzzled. Why? I had been working at First Century Bank for approximately twenty years, nine or more years of which were in that office, and I couldn't recall anything that even remotely resembled my research and definition of jasper. However, assured that the Holy Spirit was directing me, I proceeded to walk around the lobby, looking for something that might catch my attention.

From my research, I was trying to locate something green in color, preferably a translucent green. Unable to see anything that satisfied me, I started walking back to my office when my eyes fastened on a book that was on a stand near a column in the lobby. I knew this book had banking institution information in it, but I was convinced it would be a waste of time looking for jasper in it. Hesitantly, I decided that maybe I should look in the book's index for the word jasper, and, to my surprise, there it was. I turned to the article and found the exact wording I have used since when presenting "Sights and Sounds of Heaven." As you examine the following graphic, maybe you will understand, to some degree, the excitement I experienced that afternoon.

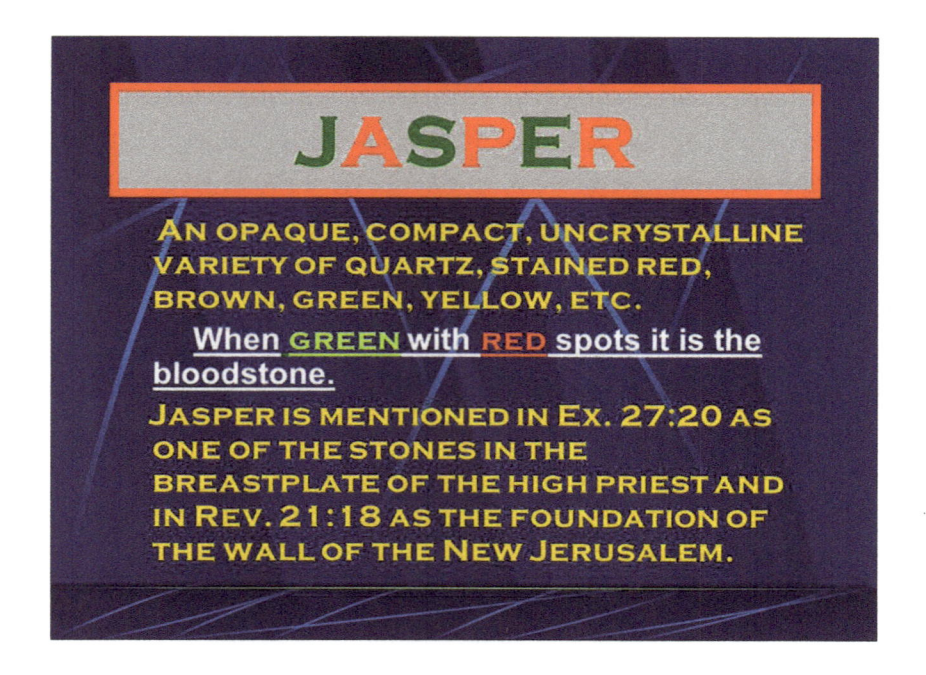

JASPER

AN OPAQUE, COMPACT, UNCRYSTALLINE VARIETY OF QUARTZ, STAINED RED, BROWN, GREEN, YELLOW, ETC.

When GREEN with RED spots it is the bloodstone.

JASPER IS MENTIONED IN EX. 27:20 AS ONE OF THE STONES IN THE BREASTPLATE OF THE HIGH PRIEST AND IN REV. 21:18 AS THE FOUNDATION OF THE WALL OF THE NEW JERUSALEM.

JASPER

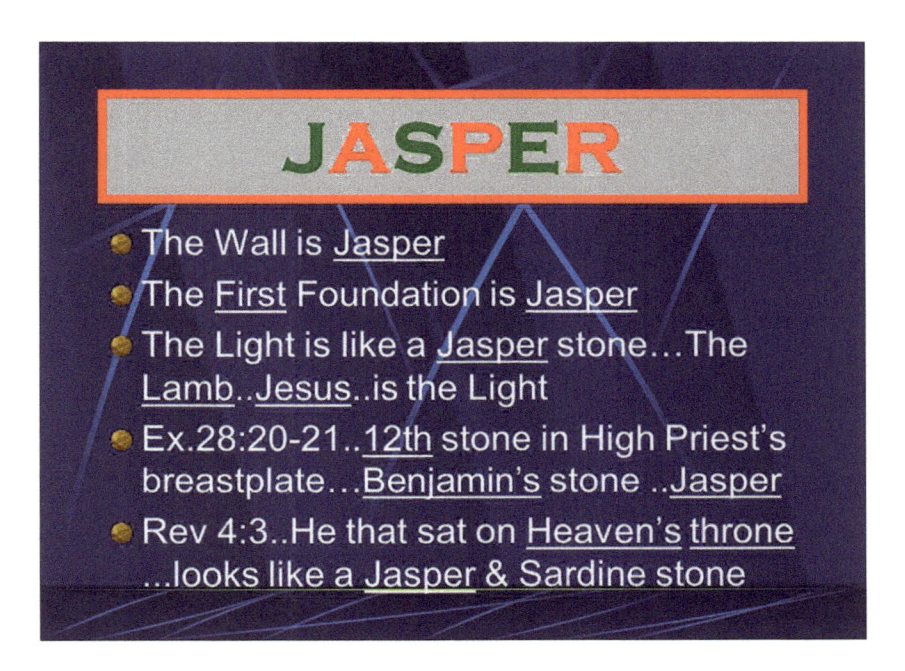

- The Wall is Jasper
- The First Foundation is Jasper
- The Light is like a Jasper stone…The Lamb..Jesus..is the Light
- Ex.28:20-21..12th stone in High Priest's breastplate…Benjamin's stone ..Jasper
- Rev 4:3..He that sat on Heaven's throne …looks like a Jasper & Sardine stone

Jasper as the Bloodstone

I had already learned that jasper was an opaque, compact, uncrystalline variety of quartz, but, I didn't know that when it has green and red spots in it, it is *the bloodstone*![60] You can't imagine how excited I felt upon my discovery of this definition of jasper. Just maybe you are now wondering why Ronnie was so excited at this finding. Almost immediately upon making my discovery, I hurriedly left the bank that afternoon. I have sincerely shared with many church congregations that I became so excited I had to leave the bank for the remainder of the day. Yes! Now you know! Sometimes I've been known to get beside myself, especially when God enlightens me about something like this, and I confess I may have shouted all over that bank lobby if I hadn't left the bank. You see, 1 Corinthians 3:11 tells us that no "other foundation can no man lay than that is laid, which is Jesus Christ." There is no other foundation, no other door, no other pathway, no amount of earth's wealth, no merit in our works or deeds, nothing you and I have done or ever will do in this life that will help us get to heaven. Jesus is the only entrance to heaven. May I repeat a scripture I quoted earlier that bears repeating: Jesus said, "I am the way, the truth, and the life: no man cometh unto the Father, but by me" (John 14:6). It is my firm opinion that the *bloodstone* is a translucent green variety of quartz with red spots in it, points us to the redeeming blood of Jesus, by which, as we ask His forgiveness sincerely, with Godly sorrow, He saves us from all past, present, and future sin. As I type these words, let me inform you that I am as excited today as I was more than fifteen years ago when I discovered jasper, in what I believe is its purest form, as *"the bloodstone."* Yes, the old, old story must continue to be told by all who know Jesus Christ in the free pardon and forgiveness of sin. A portion of the song, "Are You Washed in the Blood," says it well:

"ARE YOU WASHED IN THE BLOOD"[61]

Verse I
What can wash away my sin?
Nothing but the blood of Jesus.
What can make me whole again?
Nothing but the blood of Jesus.

Refrain
Oh, precious is the flow,
That makes me white as snow.
No other fount, I know,
Nothing but the blood of Jesus.

Verse III
When the Bridegroom cometh,
will your robes be white?
Pure and white in the blood of the Lamb?

> Will your soul be ready for the mansion bright?
> And be washed in the blood of the Lamb?
>
> Words and music by the Rev. E. A. Hoffman
> (Public domain)

I trust that as you read God's precious Word and this book, you will see why I have continued to focus on and build toward the precious stone jasper. The Holy Spirit has given us types and shadows of jasper, beginning with Benjamin's stone. I am fully aware that the light may not shine or reflect as a translucent green with red spots and that the wall and first foundation may not have those color reflections in them, but, as Jesus outshines everything in heaven, I am very sure of one thing: His *blood* will never lose its power! Thus, jasper as a bloodstone does give us a vivid picture of all Jesus did for us to give us eternal life, and I'm confident we will be constantly reminded of that in heaven.

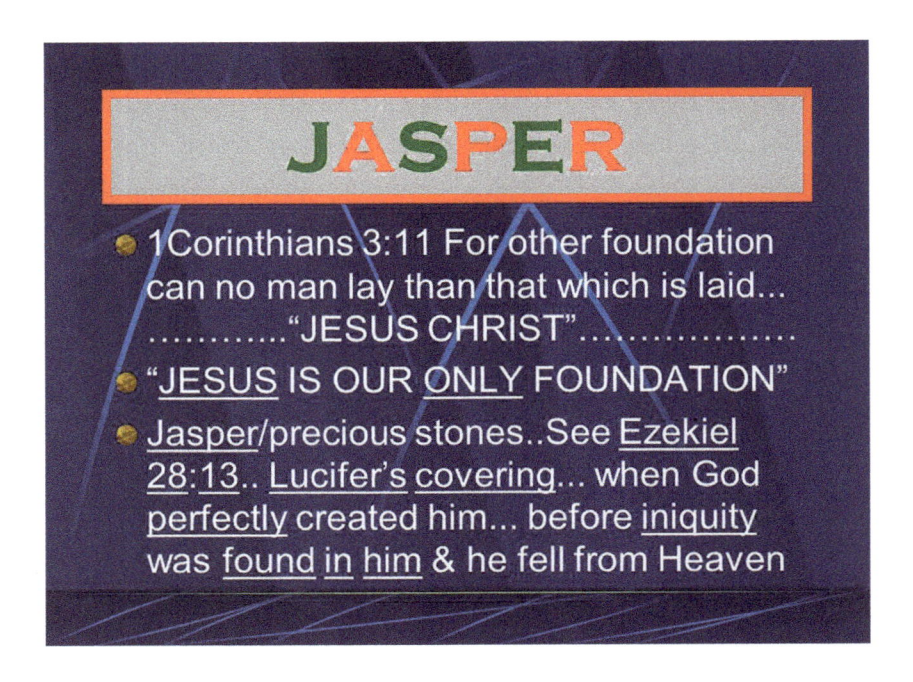

JASPER

- 1 Corinthians 3:11 For other foundation can no man lay than that which is laid... ...."JESUS CHRIST"...................
- "JESUS IS OUR ONLY FOUNDATION"
- Jasper/precious stones.. See Ezekiel 28:13.. Lucifer's covering... when God perfectly created him... before iniquity was found in him & he fell from Heaven

RONNIE S. KENNETT

When and Where Are Precious Gemstones First Mentioned in the Bible

We have discussed the twelve precious stones going back to the high priest and children of Israel in Exodus chapter 28. However, I have been amazed that many do not know when, where, and the circumstances under which these precious stones, including jasper, were first mentioned in God's Word. The scripture setting is Ezekiel 28:12–17 and Isaiah 14:12–17.

God created Lucifer as an anointed cherub, full of wisdom and perfect in beauty and every other way, and He adorned Lucifer with nine precious stones, including jasper, and even placed him in Eden, the garden of God. Many theologians and ministers believe this Eden was not the same Eden as described in Genesis. I don't find any evidence either way and choose to leave that discussion as it may be (perhaps we will find this out in heaven). Lucifer apparently had a beautiful voice, and it is thought that he led the heavenly choir in praise and worship. To think that our God, who loves us so much, created Lucifer so perfect and beautiful, covering him with nine of the precious stones and gold, and made him "light and son of the morning." I don't believe we comprehend just how much God loved Lucifer.

One day, Lucifer decided he could exalt himself above God and become like the Most High. Iniquity was found in Lucifer's heart, and like lightning, he fell and was cast out of heaven (see Isaiah chapters 12–15). How sad! We now know Lucifer as Satan, or the devil, and he desires to sift us as wheat and do everything he possibly can to destroy our lives and keep us out of heaven.

Ezekiel 28:13 mentions only nine precious gemstones that adorned Lucifer. Some theologians suggest that God had Lucifer assist with building the foundations of the new Jerusalem, and that when the ninth foundation was finished, then Lucifer sinned, and one-third of the angels fell from heaven with him. The three stones that are not listed are chrysoprasus, jacinth, and amethyst. I trust that you, as I do, see how important it is for us to humble ourselves before our holy, omnipotent Creator and commit ourselves to Him and for His service, more than ever. Let me repeat 1 Corinthians 3:11 one more time, "For other foundation can no man lay than that is laid, which is Jesus Christ." Yes, Jesus is the only foundation we need. All others either have fallen or will crumble and fall.

Benjamin: A Double Type of Jesus Christ

Genesis 35:16–19 gives the account of Rachel giving birth to Benjamin and of Rachel's death. Benjamin was Jacob's twelfth and last son. While I was researching jasper, which I document as Benjamin's stone, I thought about how difficult it must have been for Rachel and Jacob during this time. Jacob had labored fourteen years to take Rachel as his wife. He loved her so much to do that, and I believe Jacob must have thought about the years that Rachel endured before God opened her womb. I use the word *endured* respectfully, since Rachel undoubtedly suffered much seeing ten sons born to Jacob while she remained barren. Finally, God blessed Jacob and Rachel with Jacob's eleventh son, Joseph. We are well acquainted with the story of Joseph and his coat of many colors, aren't we? (Genesis, chapter 37) And now, God blesses Jacob and Rachel one more time by giving them Jacob's twelfth and last son, Benjamin.

Suddenly this beautiful love story turns tragic because, during childbirth, God takes Rachel, the wife for whom Jacob labored so long and whom he loved so much. Yet in the midst of this sad occurrence and just prior to her death, Rachel named their son "Benoni," which means "son of my sorrow." But, knowing the depth of love Jacob must have had for Rachel, he called his newborn son Benjamin, meaning, "son of my right hand."

I use this story because of the *bloodstone/jasper*, but, also, to show how Benoni and Benjamin reflect a double type and shadow of Jesus. Our Lord was the "suffering Savior," who endured the cross, shedding His lifeblood for you and me. And yet He is the "Son of the Father's right hand," for He sits at the Father's right hand, making intercession for us. What a beautiful picture Benjamin portrays of our Savior and risen Lord!

BENJAMIN

- Genesis 35:18….Rachel, as she was dying, during childbirth, named their son "BENONI" which means "son of my sorrow"…….However…….
- Jacob called him "BENJAMIN" which means "Son Of My Right Hand"……
- Thus Benjamin becomes a double type of our Savior and Lord..JESUS CHRIST

CHAPTER XVIII

THE SOUNDS OF HEAVENLY MUSIC

Heavenly Music

In Colossians 3:16, Paul exhorted the Colossian church, "Let the word of Christ dwell in you richly in all wisdom; teaching and admonishing one another in psalms and hymns and spiritual songs, singing with grace in your hearts to the Lord."

Revelation 5:9–10, "And they sang a new song, saying, Thou art worthy to take the book, and to open the seals thereof: for thou wast slain, and hast redeemed us to God by thy blood out of every kindred, and tongue, and people, and nation; and hast made us unto our God a kingdom of priests: and we shall reign on the earth."

Revelation 14:2–3, "and I heard the voice of harpers harping with their harps. And they sang as it were a new song before the throne."

My grandfather, Hubert Maynard Kennett, who went home to be with our Lord in 1934 and whom I did not have the privilege of knowing, was a pastor and music minister. My Dad told me that Grandpa traveled from church to church, teaching choirs shaped note music and hymns in four-part harmony. I still have, and treasure, the tuning fork he used to pitch the keys in which the hymns were written. I look forward to seeing him and singing with him and Dad in heaven.

When I was a youngster, my Dad taught me to play guitar (by ear, and not proficiently), and he also instilled in me that "music is a sound pleasing to the ear." My wife, Rachel, and I grew up in the coal mining community of McComas, West Virginia. McComas is still home to us, although it has changed much since the days of the coal boom of the 1940s and 1950s. We still travel now and again to our home church, now known as Crane Creek Pentecostal Holiness Church, formerly Thomas P.H. Church. Sometimes, we will sing some of the old hymns as we did many years ago. My, how we miss singing and worshipping God with so many loved ones and friends who are now in heaven! I can't wait to join them as we lift our voices in heavenly music to our God and Savior. Rachel is still playing the piano, I play guitar, and we still lead praise and worship music from time to time at our local church, South View Church.

In the late 1950s, Rachel and I, together with my brother Rev. Gene Kennett and a sister in the Lord and dear friend Joyce Devor, formed a gospel quartet known as "The Pentecostal Four." We primarily sang four-part harmony southern gospel songs, and we were blessed to sing in many churches and on regional television programs. I believe we will have four-part (or more) harmony in heaven, as we sing unto the Lord a new song, don't you? And, who knows, maybe "The Pentecostal Four" will sing a song or two.

God has blessed churches, individuals, and groups around the world, and in various languages, to praise and worship Him with music and song. How glorious heaven will be as we blend our voices with heaven's musical instruments, in praise, worship, and adoration to God the Father, Jesus Christ, and the Holy Spirit. It may be that we will harmonize, as our voices peal like thunders, in the "Four Hallelujahs" John heard in Revelation 19:1–6. Surely, the music of heaven will be glorious with "sounds pleasing to the ear." Just think about Fannie Crosby, George Beverly Shea, Bill Gaither, or Cliff Barrows leading heaven's choir. You and I will join them, and although you may be one of those I've heard say, "I can't sing or carry a tune," your voice will blend beautifully in perfect pitch. Heaven will ring with our songs of praise.

Frequently, I will ask people if they have put "their hand behind their ear" lately and listened for sounds from heaven. You may think, *wait just a minute, Ronnie, aren't you going too far now?* No, maybe I'm not going far enough. My friend, heaven is alive and active right now. The saints there are surely enjoying themselves as they await our arrival. And "if you miss me singing down here and you cannot find me anywhere, just come on over to God's heaven, for I'll be singing up there."[62]

More Sounds

We should realize that many times God is encouraging us to tune our spiritual ears to His frequency and hear "what the Spirit is saying to the churches" (Revelation 2:1—3:22). Paul tells us that Jesus invites us to "sit in heavenly places with him," before we get to heaven (Ephesians 2:6). Can we hear that great voice (perhaps God Himself) speaking in Revelation 21:3, saying, "Behold, the tabernacle of God is with men"? Hear Jesus, as Alpha and Omega, declaring, "Behold, I make all things *new*" (Revelation 21:5–8, emphasis added)? What about the river of life flowing? Can you hear it? And, John is listening as the angel describes the bride, the Lamb's wife, and the new Jerusalem (Revelation 21:9–22).

Are we listening for the sound of the kings of the earth bringing their glory and honor into the new Jerusalem (Revelation 21:24)? Can you hear the footsteps of people walking, voices of people talking, praising, singing, and even hear the people eating and drinking (Revelation 21:24–27)? Listen closely, my friend, listen. The next sound we hear may be, "Come up hither!" (Revelation 4:1).

Little Children in Heaven

We can't write about heaven unless we include our children and grandchildren and all the little children of the world. Let us remember the words of Jesus found in Mark 10:13–16, "And they brought young children to Him, that He should touch them: and His disciples rebuked those that brought them. But when Jesus saw it, He was much displeased, and said unto them, 'suffer the little children to come unto me and forbid them not: for of such is the Kingdom of God. Verily I say unto you, whosoever shall not receive the kingdom of God as a little child, he shall not enter therein.' And He took them up in His arms, put His hands upon them, and blessed them."

Children never grow up or get too mature to be very special, and occasionally, they can still use parental wisdom and guidance. After all, they are always our children. Also, Jesus reminds us that unless we are converted and become as little children, we cannot enter the kingdom of heaven (Matthew 18:1–5). Sadly, we have forgotten this in much of today's society and, to a great degree, in the church world. We have segregated the children and youth from the adults to the point where we no longer have family gatherings, as we should. Oh, that we would recall, once again, the following chorus:

"Jesus Loves the Little Children"[63]

> Jesus loves the little children,
> All the children of the world.
> Red and yellow, black and white,
> They are precious in His sight.
> Jesus loves the little children of the world.
>
> —Clare Herbert Woolston

Yes, I believe heaven will be filled with happy, vibrant, loving little children, including the more than sixty million who have been aborted before or during birth and before and after *Roe* v. *Wade*[64] in 1973. Just as heaven wouldn't be heaven without Jesus, neither would heaven be heaven without little children. By the way, I believe they will be sitting on Jesus' lap from time to time receiving His hugs and kind loving words.

I believe little children shall lead us in doing many things in heaven. You see, children and grandchildren are what make an earthly family, but because God doesn't have any grandchildren, His children will compose His heavenly family.

We have left little children out of too many things that we adults want to do. We have excluded them by being too busy to calm their fears or listen to their concerns. I think we adults, including parents, grandparents, pastors, teachers, etc., can learn much if we will take time to prayerfully consider Jesus' comments regarding "little children." To me, it's highly likely that Jesus will have activities and things for "His little children" to do in heaven that we adults can't comprehend.

Many may not agree with me concerning our children...and maybe everyone in heaven will be a certain adult age...and maybe every child will grow into adulthood...hmm...I suppose we will find out, won't we? However, I don't find enough evidence in God's Word to even suggest that heaven won't include children in its population.

Returning to sights and sounds, can you hear them rejoicing? Can you hear their laughter? Do you visualize their happy faces glowing? Do you see them basking in the love Jesus shows to each one of them, without showing favoritism? Look closely; Jesus is having a wonderful time laughing and enjoying Himself with "His little children." Writing this sure makes me want to be a little child again. Wait just a minute, Ronnie! You are His child, and so is everyone reading *Sights and Sounds of Heaven*, provided they have accepted Jesus Christ as Savior and Lord.

My, my, why did I place these words into this book about heaven? I sense it is because Jesus wants us to become more lovable and accessible than ever with/to our children, grandchildren, and all other little children. How wonderful heaven will be with God our Father, Jesus Christ our Savior and Lord, the Holy Spirit, and all of "God's children," including "His little children."

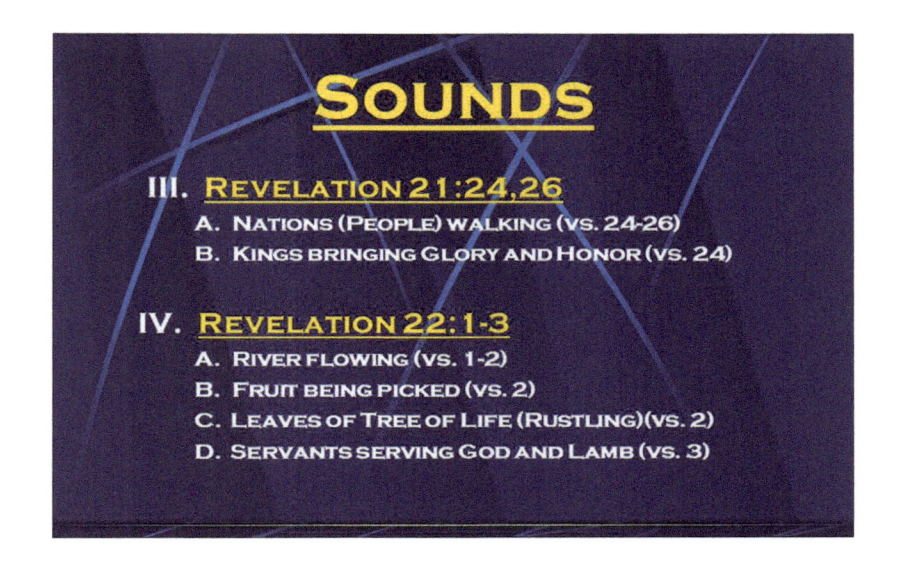

> **SOUNDS**
>
> **III. REVELATION 21:24, 26**
>   A. NATIONS (PEOPLE) WALKING (VS. 24-26)
>   B. KINGS BRINGING GLORY AND HONOR (VS. 24)
>
> **IV. REVELATION 22:1-3**
>   A. RIVER FLOWING (VS. 1-2)
>   B. FRUIT BEING PICKED (VS. 2)
>   C. LEAVES OF TREE OF LIFE (RUSTLING) (VS. 2)
>   D. SERVANTS SERVING GOD AND LAMB (VS. 3)

THE ANGELS IN HEAVEN

Are they (angels) not all ministering spirits, sent forth to minister for them who shall be heirs of salvation? (Hebrews 1:14).

In Scripture, both of the Old and New Testaments, angels are seen as that host of heavenly spirits that, according to Jewish and Christian opinion, wait upon the Triune God, who is the monarch of the universe(s), and are sent by Him to earth to execute His purposes. We define *angel* as a messenger from God, an envoy, or one who is sent.[65]

God has used angels throughout the Bible, and history and will continue to do so in eternity. In Scripture, angels are referred to as masculine, such as Gabriel and Michael. They are subject to God and Jesus Christ and always refuse to be worshipped, stressing that God alone is worthy of worship. What a contrast to the age in which we live! As a nation we exalt men and are exchanging the truth of God for a lie (Romans, chapter 1). Generally speaking, men and women are turning to the creature (mankind) for answers to life's difficulties instead of to God. Lust, greed, and lifestyles forbidden by God are happening in America with the consent of our government. It seems we have forgotten that one-third of the angels in heaven fell with Lucifer after he tried to set himself above God. These fallen angels are in chains today awaiting their final judgment.

Thankfully, God has provided guardian angels to be with us and to minister on our behalf as we serve and trust the Lord. Scripture teaches us that angels have and will continue to provide safety for God's people and execute judgment on those who choose to follow the paths of destruction, as God directs them to do so. Specific angels already have their assignments to execute the judgments that will be unleashed on earth during the great tribulation. Even then, many may refuse to accept Jesus Christ and turn from their evil ways.

Jesus said in Matthew 22:30 that there will be no marrying or giving in marriage in heaven, but we shall be as the angels of God. I believe Jesus was telling us what the angel told John when John fell at the angel's feet to worship this angel who had showed him the new Jerusalem. Revelation 22:8–9 says, "And I, John, saw these things, and heard them. And when I had heard and seen, I fell down to worship before the feet of the angel which shewed me these things. Then saith he unto me, See thou do it not: for I am thy fellowservant, and of thy brethren the prophets, and of them which keep the sayings of this book: worship God."

We know there is rejoicing in the presence of the angels, in heaven, when a sinner receives Jesus Christ as Savior and Lord. Just think about our rejoicing and worshipping God and the Lamb with them, as fellow servants, in that eternal day. Hallelujah!!

SECTION V

ETERNITY WITH GOD AND THE LAMB

CHAPTER XIX

SIGHTS AND SOUNDS OF THE TREE OF LIFE

The tree of life sitting in the new Jerusalem is beautifully described in Revelation 22:2: "In the midst of the street of it, and on either side of the river, was there the tree of life, which bare twelve manner of fruits, and yielded her fruit every month: and the leaves of the tree were for the healing of the nations."

I'm confident this is the same tree of life that God placed in the midst of the garden of Eden, since both are referred to as the tree of life. Also, remember that when Adam and Eve were driven out of Eden, God placed cherubim and a flaming sword at Eden's entrance to *keep* the way of the tree of life. The Hebrew word for *keep* is *shamar*. I have seen the word *guard* used in this verse, but I think *keep* is much more appropriate, since *shamar* can also mean "preserve or take care of";[66] and one definition, in Hebrew, for *the way of* is journey.[67] Thus Genesis 3:24 could read, "to preserve or take care of the journey of the tree of life." My point is that God didn't need a guard at Eden's entrance any more than He needs angels as guards at the twelve gates of the new Jerusalem. Furthermore, "the gates of it shall not be shut at all by day: for there shall be no night there" (Revelation 21:25). While those without the gates of the new Jerusalem will be far away and eternally lost, they will possibly know and perhaps see what is happening in heaven (see Luke 16:22–31).

I'm reminded of my childhood days and my mother preparing Sunday dinner. After dinner, Mom would cover the remaining food with a tablecloth. We would usually go to Grandma and Grandpa's house to visit for the afternoon. I remember asking Mom one Sunday why she always covered the leftover food. Her response was, "Because someone may come by to visit, and if they're hungry there's food on the table for them." By the way, we never ever locked the doors back then. I dare say that many of you also remember those days as well. Yes, people, times, and things have changed greatly; however, there is much to remember about "the good ol' days," and some traditions are worth continuing, aren't they? Today, we not only lock our doors, but we put deadbolt locks on them, and many have alarm systems installed on doors and windows to protect against burglary, robbery, etc. There will be no thieves or robbers in heaven. Heaven will surely be worth all the struggles of this life that you and I may have encountered or will ever encounter here.

I suppose, since this is my first book, it's all right for me to reminisce a little. I recall a song about the tree of life that our "Pentecostal Four" Gospel quartet used to sing called "Let Me Rest." Some of the words are:

"Let Me Rest"[68]

Verse I
There's a fountain that's free,
Flowing 'neath life's tree,
Where the saved of the earth shall rest.
It is flowing for you,

And it flows for me,
Happy souls there forever are blest.

Refrain
Let me rest 'neath the tree,
Where the fountain so pure flows by.
Where the Lamb is the light
And the souls of the saved never die.

Verse II
May we all have a right,
To the tree of life,
Standing there by the river clear.
There to rest on the banks,
Where there is no strife,
How I long, How I long to be there.

Words and music by
Joe Pannell (1929)
(Public domain)

Since the tree of life species is in the midst of the street of gold, and on both sides of the river of life, I believe there will be several trees of life that spring forth from the original tree of life, which was in the garden of Eden. My wife, Rachel, suggested there may be twelve trees on either side of the river of life and in the midst of the street leading from the throne to each of the twelve gates. The trees of would bear one manner of fruit every month on a twelve-month cycle. I don't know your favorite fruit, but mine is pineapple. However, I'm sure you or I will never have tasted any fruit like these twelve manner of fruit.

Many people have told me their favorite fruit is the apple. I've reminded them that if apples are one manner of fruit on the tree of life, they won't need to be concerned about worms in those apples. Neither will they be bruised, too ripe, or not ripe enough, and we won't find them dropping to the ground. I believe every fruit will be perfectly ripe and ready to eat.

THE LEAVES OF THE TREE OF LIFE

The leaves of the tree of life will be for the healing of the nations. Can you hear the Holy Spirit breeze blowing through the leaves? Or, better yet, can you feel the breeze? Salem Kirban says he believes living in the new Jerusalem will be one continuous time sequence of twelve-month years.[69] Although we will be living in an eternal day (no night there), we will be actively serving God and the Lamb there.

The leaves of the tree of life will be therapeutic, since the Greek word for *healing* is *therapeia*, which means "caring, serving or healing."[70] Hence, since there will be no sickness, disease, etc., there, it appears the leaves will be for the caring, serving, and therapy of the nations of the earth. It could be said that the fruit of the tree(s) will provide nutrition, and the leaves of the tree the well-being of the nations of the new earth.

There are two crucial trees mentioned in the Old Testament that I recall and two crucial trees in the New Testament. They are:

> The tree of the knowledge of good and evil (Genesis 2:17)
>
> The tree of life (Genesis 3:22)

The tree (cross) on Calvary (Acts 5:30; Galatians 3:13; 1 Peter 2:24)

The tree of life (Revelation 22:2)

It is important for me to emphasize that when Eve and Adam ate of the tree of the knowledge of good and evil, *sin and death entered the world.* I noted in chapter 1 that, after Adam and Eve were driven from the garden of Eden, God placed cherubim and a flaming sword *to keep the way of the tree of life.*

When Jesus died on the tree on Calvary, *His death conquered sin and His resurrection conquered death.* The way of the tree of life was kept, since this tree now appears in the new Jerusalem, and its fruit and leaves provide nourishment and therapies for the family of God in the new Jerusalem and on the new earth. We may eat other hidden manna, but the fruit from the tree of life will certainly be sufficient.

CHAPTER XX

SIGHTS AND SOUNDS OF THE RIVER OF LIFE

In Revelation 21:6, Jesus says, "I am Alpha and Omega, the beginning and the end. I will give unto him that is athirst of the fountain of the water of life freely." Revelation 22:1 says, "And he shewed me a pure river of water of life, clear as crystal, proceeding out of the throne of God and of the Lamb."

Just think, there will be angels to greet us at open gates that never close. The new Jerusalem's walls will echo the salvation story, and harmonious heavenly music everywhere will sound out worshipful praises to God our Father and Jesus Christ the Lamb. We will be worshiping, resting, and serving in His presence continually, in bodies that will never grow weary, as we walk on golden street, feast on fruit from the tree of life, and, let me add, sit down by the river of life.

There is nothing more peaceful than resting under a beautiful shade tree beside a flowing clear stream or river on a bright sunny day, is there? That is, unless it is resting beneath the tree of life, beside the river of life, on an eternal Son-lit day, greeting all who pass by, sharing God's love, mercy, grace, and goodness with one another, and, oh, yes, eating delicious fruit. The river of life will flow from under the throne in, at least, the directions of the golden street, if not down the center of each street.

Since Jesus uses the word *fountain*, it is likely there will be one or more beautiful water fountains, perhaps located strategically at each gate and/or near the throne area. Regardless, this is a pure, clear, flowing, life-giving river. Come to think of it, everything in the new Jerusalem and heaven will be life-giving. Hallelujah!

I'm reminded of a book written in 1898 by Rebecca Ruter Springer, originally titled *Intra Muros* (Within the Walls). The republished book title is *My Dream of Heaven*.[71] Rebecca tells of her illness, during which she lapsed into a comatose state and received a vision of heaven. At one point she meets her brother-in-law Frank, who had gone to be with the Lord several years earlier, and he is assigned to guide her on a tour through several areas of the new Jerusalem, including the river of life.

When Frank asks her to walk with him into the water, she was hesitant because she thought the water might be cold and deep and they would become submerged and wet. Frank assured Rebecca they would be fine and would breathe normally underwater. Rebecca then realized that she didn't have a towel to dry her hair with after they came out of the river, and, also, her dress would get wet. He smiled and assured her once again that everything would be all right.

Frank took Rebecca's hand and they descended into the river. Rebecca describes beautiful precious stones covering the riverbed and the refreshing, strengthening feeling that came over her as they traveled. She begins to notice how wonderful she felt in the river of life. Finally, they reached the other side and ascended out of the water. Immediately, she is amazed that her clothing and hair were dry. It was as if they had not been in the river at all. Rebecca felt so refreshed and strong. Frank reminded her that all of earth had been removed in order for her to enter heaven. After she had seen several people she had known on earth, Frank was told to return her home, and soon afterward she was healed of her illness and wrote the book of her visit to heaven.

Let me remind you, dear reader, sin and all that is of this present earth must be removed from us as well for us to enter those heavenly portals. It is truly wonderful to know that the blood of Jesus washes away all sin and that even while we are still on this earth we can "live godly in Christ Jesus" (2 Timothy 3:12), knowing that Jesus will soon return to rapture His bride, changing these earthly bodies into celestial bodies.

In that moment, possibly less than eleven-hundredths of a second, we shall forever be with our Lord. We'll worship God together on that sea of glass, and, "Over on the bright Elysian shore, where the howling tempests come no more, I'll meet you by the river."[72]

CHAPTER XXI

NO MORE CURSE

"And there shall be no more curse." (Revelation 22:3)

In this new heaven and on this new earth, the awful curse that fell upon man and upon the earth as the penalty for Adam's sin is no more (Genesis 3:14–19). Hallelujah! Paul spoke of this curse when he wrote in Romans 8:22, "For we know that the whole creation groaneth and travaileth in pain together until now." I heard a song years ago titled "The Curse Shall Be Lifted Someday."[73] Friend, that day is almost here. Jesus has broken the curse of sin, death, hell, and the grave, and He has prepared a place for us where there will be no more curse.

Serving God and the Lamb

The continuation of Revelation 22:3 reads, "but the throne of God and of the Lamb shall be in it; and His servants shall serve Him."

I have always illustrated the throne of God and the Lamb, Jesus, as being located in the center of the new Jerusalem. While the Bible doesn't pinpoint its exact setting, I like to think that the streets from all twelve gates will connect at the throne of God and the Lamb. For some reason, I believe the throne will face the center eastern gate. Of course, these are my personal opinions, and after reading the previous chapters, I'm hopeful that you understand my rationale.

I am confident that we will see Jesus seated on His throne as we gather collectively in worship, adoration, and praise to Him. Also, I believe we will have personal visits with Him in addition to "family worship" time around the throne and other locations as well. After all, we're going to be in heaven forever, my friend. In our new bodies we will never grow weary. There will be so much activity in this endless day as we serve God and Jesus, the Lamb. And for all we know, we may even explore other planets or galaxies or universes. After all, God is the Creator of everything and, as such, it seems to me that He will continue creating. Remember, our God is an awesome God!

Jesus: Alpha and Omega

In Revelation 21:6, Jesus said unto John, "It is done. I am Alpha and Omega, the beginning and the end."

Of course, alpha is the first letter and omega is the twenty-fourth and last letter of the Greek alphabet, and Jesus emphasizes the fact that He is the first and the last. He clearly lets us know He was with the Father when heaven and earth were created and that without Him was not anything made that has been made (John 1:1–5).

In Revelation 1:8 and 11, Jesus let John know that He was, He is, and He is to come, and that John was to write to the seven churches (and us) proclaiming that which was, is, and is to come. There is only one Savior, one Lord, and one coming King of kings, and His name is Jesus. There is only one message to be preached, taught, and lived, and the apostle Paul defined the gospel message in 1 Corinthians 15:2–4. That message is the gospel story of Jesus' virgin birth, His death on the old rugged cross, His burial, and His resurrection. I encourage you to read it again or, perhaps, for the first time.

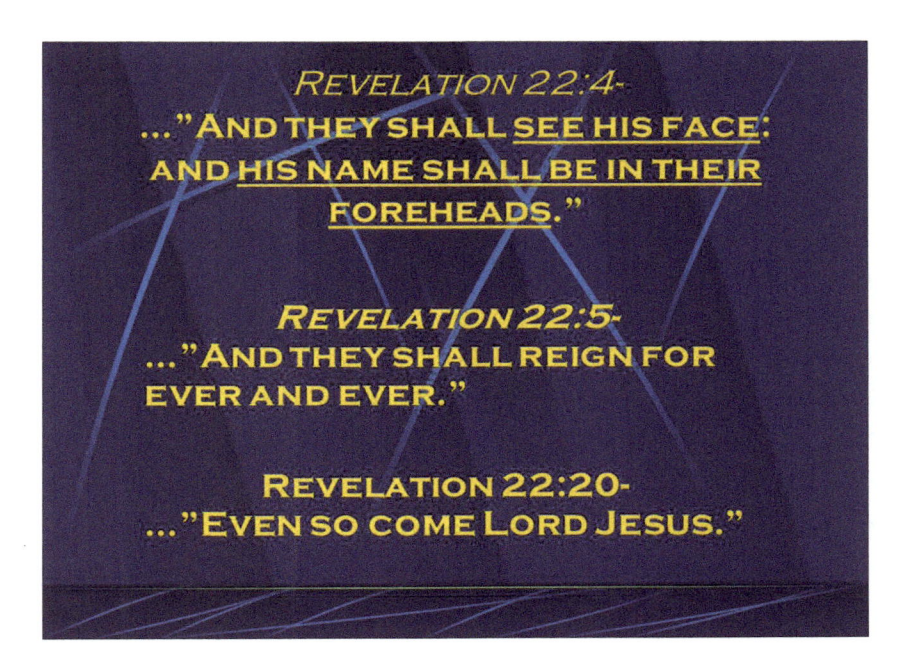

> **REVELATION 22:4-**
> ..."AND THEY SHALL SEE HIS FACE: AND HIS NAME SHALL BE IN THEIR FOREHEADS."
>
> **REVELATION 22:5-**
> ..."AND THEY SHALL REIGN FOR EVER AND EVER."
>
> **REVELATION 22:20-**
> ..."EVEN SO COME LORD JESUS."

Having read and studied the Bible over the years, I know that God's Word clearly relates several events that will take place before the events of eternity that John describes in Revelation, Chapters 21 and 22. I know we will be with Jesus from the rapture through His millennial reign on the present earth.

Also, we will be with Him, probably housed in "His Father's house," while this earth and the heavens, as they are now, are being transformed into the new heaven(s) and new earth. However, even after all of that time, I don't think words can begin to express the joy that will be ours when we see our blessed Savior's face, as He sits on His throne in the new Jerusalem as eternity with Him begins. I would not attempt to describe how we will react. Oh, I'm sure some think they will talk with Him and ask Him several questions. Others may wonder: "Is this what I expected Jesus to look like?"

Do you have an opinion as to how you may address our Savior, the Lamb of God, and our King of kings and Lord of lords, Jesus

Christ, when we first see Him? I believe we will be speechless and bow (or fall) before Him in worship. It may be some time before we can rise or speak.

After all, Revelation 1:17 describes John's reaction when he saw Jesus. John fell before Him as a dead man. John could only rise to his feet after Jesus laid His right hand on his shoulder and told him not to fear. This is John who was one of the twelve apostles. The same John traveled with Jesus for three and a half years, was known as the closest disciple to Jesus, and was assigned to take care of Mary, Jesus' mother. Yet he couldn't stand in the Lord's presence. I hardly think we will be able to either. We will probably bask in His glory for some time after we hear, "Well done. Welcome home."

However, we'll have plenty of heavenly *kairos* time, won't we? I feel certain we will tell the story "saved by His grace" at some later time. As Savior and Lord, He is all God's precious Word portrays Him to be, and in eternity Jesus will reign as "the Lamb." He shall put His name in our foreheads. I don't know if this name will be Jesus Christ, or Alpha and Omega, or Lamb of God, or His new name (see Revelation 3:12). The important thing is we shall wear His name and serve Him forever. Just think; we will be enjoying eternity worshipping, serving, and reigning with God our Father, Jesus Christ the Son, and the Holy Spirit. How glorious the thought!

Rachel and I were married by our Pastor, the Rev. Albert McGhee, at Crane Creek Pentecostal Holiness Church on December 6, 1958. At this writing we have been married sixty-one blessed years. We will never forget that special day, nor will we forget many other things about Pastor McGhee. He loved music, and there were two songs he loved to sing. One hymn was "The Pearly White City."[74]

SIGHTS AND SOUNDS OF HEAVEN

The other was entitled "Saved by Grace." In my mind, I can hear him singing those beautiful words as I pen them:

SAVED BY GRACE[75]

Verse I
Some day the silver cord will break,
And I no more as now shall sing.
But, oh the joy when I awake,
Within the palace of the King.

Refrain
And I shall see Him face to face,
And tell the story, saved by grace.
And I shall see Him face to face,
And tell the story, saved by grace.

Verse II
Some day till then, I'll watch and wait
My lamp all trimmed and burning bright.
That when my Savior opens the gate,
My soul to Him may take its flight.

Words Fanny J. Crosby (1892)
Music George C. Stebbins (1894)
(Public domain)

Today, many people proudly wear the colors of their favorite sports teams. In politics there are buttons, hats, and banners promoting their support for certain candidates or parties. There is the roar of the crowds as they root for their favorites, such as presidents, kings, queens, sports figures, Hollywood celebrities, TV personalities, etc.

Even in the "church world," people have their favorite preachers, sermons, songs, and they get excited upon meeting those who preach or sing well. While all of that is probably all right, we need to commend and exhort everyone who has answered God's call to serve. I expect we will be pleasantly surprised when we see people in heaven, we were not sure would "make it." Oops! Maybe we should concentrate on serving God in the ministry area(s) to which we have been called and let God do the calling, sending, and judging.

We live in a world, including America, where many don't want to ever hear the name "Jesus" anymore, let alone see Him face-to-face. Traveling from church to church and city to city, I am greatly concerned as to how much we really desire to see Jesus. A valid question may be, "Just how popular is Jesus in your world?" I mean in your life, your family and home, your church, your workplace, and your community? You see, we are rapidly deleting church services from our schedules to make time for sports and other events; some pastors, church boards, and congregations are only having one service per week; and revivals are now scheduled for one day or no more than three-day service events. I guess I'm meddling, but it seems like we just don't have much time for Jesus anymore, or, as the liberal media tells us, I'm out of touch with the times we live in today. My great concern is that while we preach and teach that Jesus is coming very soon, and He is, yet, we are shrinking our regular church services, revivals, and evangelistic outreaches.

Since his fall, Satan has always tried to imitate God and Jesus. He will deceive people during the tribulation by having the false prophet place the antichrist's name in people's foreheads. He will again try to counterfeit what he thinks Jesus will do in heaven. In that time, many will be deceived. However, when Jesus places His name in our foreheads (Revelation 22:4), it may be that Satan, the antichrist, the false prophet, and all who refused to accept Jesus Christ will be seeing this event take place from the lake of fire, the second death abode. How tragic this will be for all who have rejected our Lord!

CHAPTER XXII

NO MORE NIGHT AND SUPER SUNDAY

> "And there shall be no night there; and they need no candle, neither light of the sun; for the Lord God giveth them light: and they shall reign for ever and ever." (Revelation 22:5).

I really enjoy daylight saving time. Yes, the "spring forward" in March takes getting used to each year, as does the "fall back" in November. But if you're like I am, you certainly enjoy longer daylight hours. Also, we don't have enough hours in the day anymore, do we? Making the most of each day has turned into a "rat race," I hear many people say. How about your life? Is it a struggle to get things done anymore? Could it be that we just need to readjust our priorities? But this book isn't about questions like these, or is it?

I remember hearing a great analogy once regarding our time and our priorities in life. J. Vernon McGee, producer of the radio ministry "Thru the Bible,"[76] once said that Christians should be like a "good watch." We should be pure gold, open-faced, always on time, well-regulated, and full of good works. Without any doubt, this practice will help each of us make the most of our time every day of our lives.

Being in the service of our Lord is all about evangelizing this world, doing good and putting into practice "the Good Samaritan principle" (Luke 10:29–37). In John 9:4, Jesus said, "I must work the works of Him that sent me, while it is day: the night cometh, when no man can work." We must hasten to work in His vineyard because this dispensation of grace soon will end, and the dreadful night of great tribulation and Armageddon will commence on this earth. As Christians we will be safe, but let us work His works to bring the lost to Jesus Christ before it is too late. Let us prepare for...

No more night! One eternal day! Wow! I'm wondering how some of us will handle this. I can hear someone saying, "When will I get any sleep? I must have my rest!" And besides that, "What are we going to be doing for all eternity anyway?" The answer to those questions is that we will have new bodies that will never grow weary and will be forever in His presence serving God and the Lamb. I have already given you my thoughts on darkness, shadows, blackness of night, etc. You see, no more night also means that all the wicked things of this sin-cursed world that were done under the cover of night and darkness will forever be erased from us in heaven.

Perhaps you are in physical darkness, and someone is reading these words to you because some disease blinded your physical eyes. Let me pause to encourage you by reminding you that not only will God wipe all tears from your eyes, but you will also see perfectly in that eternal day. Seeing Jesus will be worth it all, but you will also see all of the beauty of heaven. There will never be any darkness for you again. No more night! Praise the Lord!

Why will there be no more night? Not only because the Bible tells us so, but Jesus will outshine everything else in the new

Jerusalem and on the new earth. My brother, the Reverend Gene Kennett, recorded a gospel song titled "Jesus Will Outshine Them All," which was written by Gordon Jensen in 1972. It emphasizes Revelation 21:23–24, for the Lamb will be the light of the city and the nations of the earth shall walk in the light of it.

"Jesus Will Outshine Them All"[77]

Verse I
Oh, what glory awaits me in heaven's bright city,
When I get there such sights I'll behold!
A million scenes of rare beauty will demand that I view them,
Still Jesus will outshine them all!

Refrain
Mansions will glisten on the hills of glory,
Happy reunions on streets of gold,
Angel choirs singing glad praises forever,
But Jesus will outshine them all.

Verse II
The sparkling river is flowing, happy faces all glowing,
Land of splendor where night never falls;
The golden glass gives reflection to that city's perfection,
Still Jesus will outshine them all.

—By Gordon Jenson

Super Sunday

In the early 1970s on a Saturday afternoon, I was studying to speak the following day at a church in Princeton, West Virginia. The professional football season had ended, and playoffs had begun to determine the teams for the Super Bowl. I had the television on and noticed that every other commercial was centered on the Super Bowl. I vividly recall commenting to myself that God will also have a "Super Sunday" someday and that someone should write a song about His Super Sunday. Almost immediately, I felt prompted by the Holy Spirit to do just that. My wife, Rachel, came in the room, and I asked her to bring me a pen and some paper because I felt like writing a song. In the space of approximately thirty minutes, I had written the following song:

"SUPER SUNDAY"[78]

Verse I
People talk about the Super Bowl,
And baseball's World Series.
All kinds of entertainment,
This mortal man to please.
Now, maybe some of that's all right,
For the price we have to pay.
But, if we don't put Jesus first,
We'll miss His Super Sunday.

Refrain
We'll have a Super Sunday,
When Jesus takes us home.
A Super "Duper" Sunday,
Over heaven we will roam.
What a hallelujah meeting,
Around the throne,
On the crystal sea,
On that Super Sunday,
In God's eternity.

SIGHTS AND SOUNDS OF HEAVEN

> Verse II
> Yes, even in the church today,
> Folks want to be entertained.
> If we don't, so many say,
> I just won't go back there again.
> But, if we will only worship God,
> In the good old-fashioned way.
> He will hear our cry,
> And He'll satisfy,
> All the way to Super Sunday.
>
> Words and music by Ronnie S. Kennett

God's Word teaches us, and I have just reminded you, of that eternal, unending day. I love to think of that day as one "Super Sunday."

Remember what happened after God had finished His work on that sixth day. He rested on the seventh day. God is so good to us that He gave man a seventh day, set aside for rest and worship (not that we shouldn't worship Him every day). Come to think of it, we have sure made a mess of this day of rest, haven't we? We stay so busy we don't have time to do much except work, work, work, play, play, play, become bored, and complain.

Many people are so preoccupied that they can't seem to find time for family, church, or, oh yes, God. God longs for His masterpiece, that's you and me, to worship Him, in spirit and in truth (John 4:24). He desires that we fellowship and dine with Him as well.

I recall a former pastor, the Rev. Alex Day, sharing a personal story with me concerning spending more time with the Lord.

> Rev. Day said, "The Holy Spirit convicted me that I wasn't devoting enough time for prayer, fellowship, and dining with the Lord." He continued, "Ronnie, I began setting aside one day a week to spend several hours alone with God. I took a loaf of bread and bottle of grape juice, and as the Lord and I communed together, I would partake of the Lord's Supper (communion)." He added, "Those times with the Lord changed my life and my ministry."

You and I may not spend time with God in the manner Brother Day did; however, I'm more convinced than ever that I do need to spend more time with Him. How about you? In that eternal day His people, called by His name, will do just that, and I can assure you, it won't be boring.

CHAPTER XXIII

REIGNING FOREVER WITH GOD THE FATHER, JESUS CHRIST THE SON, AND THE HOLY SPIRIT

"and they shall reign for ever and ever" (Revelation 22:5).

The word *they* refers to all who are in Christ, and *ever and ever* means unto the ages of ages. Can you comprehend this statement? I cannot! You see, Paul tells us in 1 Corinthians 7:22, "For he that is called in the Lord, being a servant, is the Lord's freeman" or bond slave. We are servants of the Lord, and we will serve Him in heaven, yet we shall "reign with Him." Wow! What a wonderful Savior!

I have worked at various jobs, held several positions, and served on many boards during my life, and perhaps many who read this book may have done so as well. I have labored for some individuals who demanded more than a day's work for a small paycheck, and some who were very considerate of their employees and who paid a fair day's wages. I have always believed in the "team" concept and tried to teach "cross-training." Some employees who worked under my supervision tried to convince me they had "skilled labor" positions and should not be asked to help others, while some team members were willing to assist other team members when needed. May I tell you that working together as a team makes for a much better workplace. I'm sure there are many who believe there will be "skilled labor" positions in heaven. I am confident we will enjoy serving God and the Lamb (Jesus), and any position we hold in His kingdom, during the one-thousand-year kingdom age and in heaven, will be wonderful, and the pay will be "out of this world."

You may think it strange for me to include the above comments in this section, since we are discussing "reigning" with Christ in heaven. The Greek word for *reign* is *symbasileuo*, which metaphorically means "to possess supreme honor, liberty, and blessedness, with one in the kingdom of God."[79] I have always put into practice the saying, "The ground is level at Calvary." In laymen's terms, everyone who accepts Jesus Christ as Savior and Lord has equal status in the kingdom of God. There are no "big I" and "little you" children of God. I know that all Christians will appear at the judgment seat of Christ to be judged for the deeds done in our earthly body. It is very likely at this time that Jesus will designate certain leadership positions, placing certain people over cities or areas of the earth, since we will rule and reign with Christ during the millennial reign.

The apostle Paul said, "We are saved unto good works" (Ephesians 2:10; 2 Timothy 3:17). And, as Christians and overcomers, we will receive various crowns and rewards for the works done in this life, after we have accepted Jesus Christ as Savior and Lord. The Bible lists five specific crowns in which all overcomers who love Christ and His appearing may share. These are:
1. A crown of life (James 1:12)
2. A crown of righteousness (2 Timothy 4:8)

3. A crown of glory (1 Peter 5:4)
4. A crown of rejoicing soul winners (1 Thessalonians 2:19)
5. A crown of martyrs (Revelation 2:10)

Upon receiving these crowns, we will cast them at Jesus' feet, for He alone is worthy to receive honor and glory and power. The only worthiness and righteousness we have is because of Jesus.

Yes, we will be supremely honored, blessed, and given the liberty to share together the continual joy, peace, glory, and splendor of the new Jerusalem and all of heaven as we worship and serve God and the Lamb. I hope I sound excited because I am, aren't you?

Behold I Come Quickly

"Behold, I come quickly." (Revelation 22:7)

"behold, I come quickly." (Revelation 22:12)

"Surely I come quickly." Revelation 22:20)

Jesus speaks these words three times in the final chapter of Revelation. They should ring clearly in our hearts, knowing that we, as believers, are on the brink of the rapture of His church. Skeptics, scoffers, atheists, satanists, the liberal media, unbelieving politicians, and others may attempt to change God's Word to satisfy their whims and fit their agendas, but all of that won't delay the catching away of His bride. He could return at any moment.

Not one more prophecy requires fulfillment before Jesus comes to take His children home. His warnings are to all nations of the earth. This includes those who have read His Word and/or heard it preached or taught. These warnings are clear and precise. His gospel has been and continues to be proclaimed through prophets, apostles, evangelists, pastors, teachers, missionaries, and believers all over the earth. His church must continue sounding out the gospel message so that "whosoever will" may come to Jesus and drink of the water of life freely.

Although we live in perilous and uncertain times, I believe we also live in the most exciting era in history. Jesus said in Matthew 24:33, "So likewise ye, when ye shall see all these things, know that it is near, even at the doors," and again, in Luke 21:28, "And when these things begin to come to pass, then look up, and lift up your heads; for your redemption draweth nigh." I encourage you to prayerfully read Matthew (chapter 21), Mark (chapters 13 and 17), and Luke (chapter 21). The prophecies contained in these chapters, together with many other scriptures, all point to Jesus' soon return.

America's current economic crisis, which is affecting the entire world, is placing us on the brink of a "one world government." The catastrophic occurrences in the earth and seas, including earthquakes, tornadoes, floods, and other natural disasters should be warnings that God isn't pleased with our manmade ideology. We have become obsessed with global warming, and while man has done things to harm the earth and atmosphere, we are also forgetting that only God has nature and the elements under His control.

Many of our elected leaders are determined to satisfy personal selfish agendas that intentionally cause us to stray from the foundations set forth by our forefathers. Just in the past fifty years, our United States Supreme Court has removed prayer and Bible reading from our schools and allowed abortion on demand, thereby killing unborn children by the millions. At this writing more than sixty million babies have been aborted in the United States alone. We have actually lost a generation of our children. The Ten

Commandments and manger scenes depicting the birth of Jesus Christ are no longer allowed in public places, primarily because a few people may be offended.

Individual states now permit same-sex marriages, and some churches allow homosexual or lesbian clergy in their pulpits. Yes, God loves everyone and sent His only begotten Son to die for every person. His love reaches to every person who will accept Jesus Christ as Savior and Lord, including the homosexual and lesbian. However, His Word is clear; same-sex marriages and homosexual and lesbian practices are sinful, and those who live in and try to justify such lifestyles must realize the consequences of continuing in such lustful desires and practices.

The apostle Paul declared in Romans 1:24–27,

> Wherefore God also gave them up to uncleanness through the lusts of their own hearts, to dishonor their own bodies between themselves: who changed the truth of God into a lie, and worshipped and served the creature more than the Creator, who is blessed forever. Amen. For this cause God gave them up unto vile affections: for even their women did change the natural use into that which is against nature; and likewise the men, leaving the natural use of the woman, burned in their lust one toward one another; men with men working that which is unseemly, and receiving in themselves that recompense of their error which was meet.

May I strongly suggest that you read the first and second chapters of Romans if you haven't done so recently. It, along with many other scriptures, confirms that God's Word is unchanging. He will not allow one jot or tittle of it to be changed so that we may satisfy our fleshly and worldly desires.

America is the land of the free and the home of the brave, and our people(s) have a right to their individual beliefs. However, America is still "one nation under God,"[80] and the vast majority of Americans believe and adhere to the principles upon which our nation was founded. Our forefathers framed our founding documents based upon the Bible, God's infallible Word. We have been warned by God's Word in Psalm 9:17, "The wicked shall be turned into hell, and all the nations that forget God." Isaiah 60:12 says, "For the nation and kingdom that will not serve thee [God] shall perish; yea, those nations shall be utterly wasted."

Why have I included this chapter in a book about heaven? Because God is *love* (1 John 4:8), and His desire is that all of us accept Jesus Christ as His Son and our Savior and Lord. God has promised eternal life to all overcomers. God is longsuffering, and it is His will that none perish (2 Peter 3:9) but that all come to repentance and live with Him forever in heaven. Hell has been prepared for the devil and his angels, and the only additional people who will be eternally lost, separated from God, and suffering eternal agony will be those who have already or will reject Jesus Christ.

It is vital that I point out to you that, in the midst of John's description concerning the new Jerusalem and the new heaven, he includes Revelation 21:8, where Jesus Himself lists those who will be eternally lost and who won't be with Him in the new Jerusalem and heaven. This verse states:

> But the fearful, and unbelieving, and the abominable, and murderers, and whoremongers, and sorcerers, and idolaters, and all liars, shall have their part in

the lake which burneth with fire and brimstone: which is the second death.

Jesus emphasizes this again in Revelation 22:15. While God loves everyone in the world, He will not compromise His Word, nor will He honor peoples and nations who reject Him or turn from Him.

Reunion in Heaven

Rachel and I, together with our children and grandchildren and other family members, look forward to our family reunions. We greatly miss our parents, grandparents, siblings, other family members, friends, and brothers and sisters in Christ who are now in heaven with Jesus awaiting our coronation day. We continue our family reunions with siblings, children, grandchildren, and extended family members and anxiously look forward to them each year. I'm sure many of you reading *Sights and Sounds* echo our anticipation.

Of course, we greet one another with hugs and kisses, reminisce with precious memories, enjoy fellowship, games and laughter, update each other on current happenings, share pictures, sing, pray, and give thanks to the Lord for one another, and—oh yes—we eat, and eat, and eat! After getting to this point in writing this book, I simply want to reinforce how glorious our reunion in heaven will be. One thing is sure, God's family should be and certainly will be "one big happy family" in heaven.

The rapture of Christ's bride is imminent. Jesus is coming soon, and we will join the ransomed around His throne on that sea of glass. Yes, we'll walk on golden streets, sit by the river of life and eat fruit from the tree of life. We will greet one another, perhaps with hugs and... oops, here I go sounding so much like family reunion time again.

This earth has been here for six thousand years or more. The beginning—the garden of Eden (Paradise) and Adam and Eve—seem to many people to be fables, tales told, untrue and unreal events, or just a distant part of history. However, to all of us who have experienced, and are experiencing the love of God through Jesus Christ, that beginning points and leads to heaven.

You see, we must believe the entirety of the Bible as God's Word, written under the inspiration of the Holy Spirit by holy men. We must believe that God's Son, Jesus, came to this earth from heaven, was born of the Virgin Mary and was crucified, suffering and dying in agony on the cross to redeem us from sin. We must believe that Jesus rose again the third day as the Resurrection and the Life. And now, Jesus has gone to prepare a place for all who accept Him as Savior and Lord and will return very soon to "catch away His bride."

We are currently living in the dispensation of grace. God has His timetable for man to live on this earth and for this heaven and earth as they exist today. His Word clearly outlines the future order of events.

I strongly believe the next great event to take place is the rapture of the church. After that wonderful event, the seven-year great tribulation will begin. Immediately thereafter, Jesus' second coming will occur, and every person living on earth at that time will see Jesus coming in the clouds of heaven. The battle of Armageddon will take place, the antichrist and false prophet will be cast into the lake of fire, and Satan will be bound in the bottomless pit for one thousand years. Jesus will then begin His millennial reign on earth, and all who have part in the first resurrection will reign with Him. How glorious that will be! Then, God will loose Satan for a short period of time, the battle of Gog and Magog will take place, and Satan will be cast into the lake of fire, where the antichrist and false prophet have been for one thousand years.

After the millennial reign and the other events noted above are finished, the current heaven(s), which have existed from Genesis 1:1, will pass away with a great noise, and the elements will melt with fervent heat. The present earth and the works therein shall be burned up, and all these things shall be dissolved (2 Peter 3:10–11).

The great white throne judgement will take place, during which the wicked dead from all generations, beginning with Adam and Eve, will be judged, and every person whose name is not found written in the Lamb's book of life will be cast into the lake of fire, which is the second death. While there are those who believe this death will be an instantaneous, final death similar to the physical death of the body that we are accustomed to, God's Word is very emphatic. This second death will be everlasting torment in an eternal lake of fire, where "the worm dieth not and the fire is not quenched" (Mark 9:42–48). Jesus gave this warning three times in this same chapter of Mark. Let me hasten to say that, while this judgment must take place, it is God's will for every human being to be saved.

Immediately after God's white throne judgement ends, eternity begins and will never end. Just as we have viewed and heard the sights and sounds of the new heaven and the new Jerusalem in this book, there will also be the new earth.

The New Earth

> "And I saw a new heaven and a new earth for the first heaven and the first earth were passed away; and there was no more sea" (Revelation 21:1).

Isn't it interesting that recently many have become so concerned that global warming, pollution, rain forest, and other vegetation concerns, earthquakes, pestilences, etc., are destroying our planet? Some people have become very wealthy trying to convince us that the earth's climate may get too hot, the sun become too cold, or pollution may overtake us and other environmental concerns. Who would have thought twenty years ago that we would be buying bottled water to drink? We can recite valid reasons to give us concern so we will become more prudent in our care for this first earth God has given us.

It seems to me that mankind has forgotten one very important fact. God made this first heaven and first earth, and God alone will dissolve them. Only He will make them pass away as He creates a new heaven and a new earth. We should remind ourselves that previously referenced scriptures from 2 Peter 3:10–14 clearly inform us that our planet earth will be burned up, including everything in it. Beginning with the fall of Adam and Eve in the garden of Eden, when God placed a curse on the ground, even the earth is groaning, to be delivered/released from the bondage of corruption man has brought about because of sin (see Romans 8:18–25 and Genesis 3:1–17).

What a glorious hope we have, knowing that God will cleanse all impurities from this first earth and in the heavens. Man may continue to desecrate and destroy because of their moral corruption, decay, depravity, wickedness, other sinful pleasures, wars, and other manners of evil and greed, but God will have the final say. He will renew this earth, wherein the nations of His saved people(s) will serve Him in righteousness. We know from His Word that the kings of the new earth will bring their glory and honor into the new Jerusalem (Revelation 21:23–24).

There are many questions concerning this new earth that can be and are being asked. Biblical research conducted by me and others confirm that many of these questions are not clearly answered by the Bible. However, they are noteworthy and fine for discussion and prayerful consideration, in my opinion. Some questions I have often been asked, and have asked myself, include the following:

Will the new earth be similar to the garden of Eden?

I can only say that the new earth will be "Paradise."

Who will serve as kings governing the new earth?

I have no idea who will be assigned; however, "we all will serve God and the Lamb" (Revelation 22:5).

How large will the new earth be?

Some believe the new earth will be as large as Saturn. All I am sure of is the earth will "abide forever." Personally, I believe it will remain the size it is now. Today, there are more than seven billion people living on the earth. The new Jerusalem will easily accommodate several billion as well, and all of the bride of Christ will live there. Maybe God will enlarge the size of the new earth, but since His Word doesn't give an answer, neither will I attempt to do so.

Will those living on the new earth have glorified bodies or earthly bodies?

Some believe and teach that the inhabitants of the new earth will live in earthly bodies that will be immortal and never decay or die. They base this on the fact that the earth's inhabitants still living at the end of the tribulation period and after the battle of Armageddon will continue living in earthly bodies during the millennial reign of Jesus Christ on the earth, and thus, those who accept and follow Jesus Christ during the millennial reign will retain their earthly bodies as they enter into eternity. They contend that these earthly bodies will be similar to the bodies Adam and Eve had in the garden of Eden before sin entered the world. Of course, although Adam's body was made from the dust of the first earth, God drove Adam and Eve out of the garden of Eden "lest they partook of the tree of life and live forever" (my words) in an earthly body. I personally think the people living on the new earth will have the same kind of glorified body Jesus and those living in the new Jerusalem will have.

It is interesting to note that Adam lived to the age of nine hundred and thirty years before he died (Genesis 5:5). I have heard some ministers say they aren't sure Adam was saved, since the Bible doesn't indicate or say that Adam didn't repent or ask God to forgive him and Eve. Think about that! Adam was made from the dust of the earth, and Eve was made from Adam's rib. Adam walked and talked with God in the cool of the day. Eve talked with the serpent, Satan, and yet both may be lost without God?! I suppose we will never know. Why not? Revelation 21:4 explains that "the former things are passed away."

I have always taught and continue to believe that every person in heaven, regardless of whether they live in the new Jerusalem or on the new earth, will have glorified bodies. Some people believe that *only* those living in the new Jerusalem (the bride of Christ) will live in glorified bodies. If they are correct and if those living on the new earth will live in earthly bodies, then I need to ask the following question:

Where will the people who are born during the millennium and who accepted Jesus Christ as Savior be housed (live) during the white throne judgment and the transformation from the first earth to the new earth?

If the millennial saints retain earthly bodies, I don't believe they can inhabit the new Jerusalem while the first earth is being cleansed because they are made from the dust of the earth and have been tainted by sin. Haven't they?

2 Peter 3:10–13 tells us,

> But the day of the Lord will come as a thief in the night; in the which the heavens shall pass away with a great noise, and the elements shall melt with fervent heat, the earth also and the works that are therein shall be burned up. Seeing then that all these things shall be dissolved, what manner of persons ought you to be in all holy conversation and godliness, looking for and hastening unto the coming of the day of the Lord, wherein the heavens being on fire shall be dissolved, and the elements shall melt with fervent heat. Nevertheless, we, according to His promise, look for new heavens and a new earth, wherein dwelleth righteousness.

I believe that during the millennium, saints will have glorified immortal bodies like Jesus' glorified body and like those whose bodies of the bride, which will be changed during the rapture. Certainly, there will be perpetual generations on the new earth as are mentioned in Genesis 9:8–12 when God made His covenant with Noah.

Will there be marriages and children born on the new earth?

Some people believe there will be marriages and children born on the new earth, in eternity. In my opinion, God's Word is ambiguous concerning many matters; however, I certainly don't believe this will happen in heaven.

I do believe the new earth will be a paradise as was Eden. Why? God and the Lamb (Jesus Christ) will be the light continuously illuminating the earth. I am a wait-and-see person regarding some of these questions and simply know our Lord has His plan, purpose, and design to which He hasn't given us the answers yet.

Just as John saw, we shall behold new heavens(s) and a new earth, which God will have created and wherein dwelleth righteousness. We shall enjoy living forever and ever serving God and Jesus, the Lamb, as we partake of all of the "sights and sounds of heaven."

My question to you as I close *Sights and Sounds of Heaven* is: Where will you spend eternity? My prayer is that you already have or will now choose Jesus Christ as your Savior and Lord.

As for me and my house, we choose Jesus Christ...and as Abraham said, we are "looking for a City" which hath foundations: That city is the new Jerusalem, and I conclude with the following hymn:

"THE PEARLY WHITE CITY"[81]

Verse I
There's a holy and beautiful city, whose builder and ruler is God.
John saw it descending from heaven, when Patmos, in exile he trod.
Its high massive wall is of jasper, the city itself is pure gold,
And when my frail here is folded, mine eyes shall its glory behold.

Refrain
In that bright city, pearly white city,
I have a mansion, a harp and a crown.
Now I am watching, waiting and longing,
For the white city that's soon coming down.

Verse II
No sin is allowed in that city, and nothing defiling nor mean.
No pain and no sickness can enter, no crape on the doorknob is seen.
Earth's sorrows and cares are forgotten, no tempter is there to annoy:
No parting words ever are spoken, there's nothing to hurt and destroy.

Verse III
No heartaches are known in that city, no tears ever moisten the eye.
There's no disappointment in heaven, no envy and strife in the sky.
The saints are all sanctified holy, they live in sweet harmony there;
My heart now is set on that city, and some day its blessings I'll share.

continued

Verse IV
My loved ones are gathering yonder, my friends, too, are passing away.
And soon I shall join their bright number, and dwell in eternity's day.
They're safe now in glory with Jesus, their trials and battles are past;
They overcame sin and the tempter, They've reached that fair city at last.

Copyright 1929, by Arthur F. Ingler.
Renewed by Nazarene Pub.House, Owner (Public domain)

Ronnie S. Kennett

SPECIAL NOTE OF THANKS

<u>XULON</u>
All of those who have assisted in any way –
Thank you to all of the Xulon Staff.

<u>RITA BENNETT</u>
"To Ronnie Kennett; Several of the seven pictures from Heaven Tours"; courtesy to use from: Rita M. Bennett, author, copyright 2009, president, Christian Renewal Association, P. O. Box 576, Edmonds, WA 98020 USA."

Graphic #12—The Majestic Throne of God
Graphic #21—Map of the New Jerusalem
Graphic #29 – The Tunnel of Light into Heaven

For more information relating to the illustrations of heaven from author Rita Bennett's book Heaven Tours *(in cooperation with Bridge-Logos Publishing), see her web site www.EmotionallyFree.org.*

<u>PAT MARVENKO SMITH</u>
Revelation Productions
www.revelationillustrated.com
Graphic #11—The Burning Bush

Graphic #15—New Jerusalem
Graphic #24—The Rapture
Graphic #25—Emerald Throne City
Graphic #26—King of Kings and Lord of Lords
Graphic #30—Foundations of the City

<u>JACKSON B. "JACK" KENNETT</u>
Instagram: jkennet51
Graphic #2—The Rainbow and Noah's Ark

Also, featured on back cover

<u>DAVID MCNEIL</u>
Author Photo and Graphics Organization

GRUBB PHOTO
1316 Bland Street
Bluefield, WV 24701
www.grubbphoto.com

Endnotes

1. Lehman, F. M. *The Love of God*. Copyright 1917, renewed 1945, by F. M. Lehman, assigned to Nazarene Publishing House; music by F. M. Lehman, arr. by Claudia Lehman Mays. Arr. #2 listed as Public Domain. Accessed 14 Dec. 2019 https://www.pdhymns.com/pdh_main_T.htm..

2. Church Hymnal, page 220. Copyright 1951, renewal, 1979, by Tennessee Music and Printing Company, Cleveland, Tennessee.

ACKNOWLEDGMENTS
FOREWORD
PREFACE
INTRODUCTION

SECTION I
IN THE BEGINNING

3. Kennett, Ronnie S. *The Heavenly Way*. 1959.

4. Salem Kirban Reference Bible (1979), copyright #79-53475, page 478 (excerpted).

5. "Apollo 11: First Men on the Moon." Nola Taylor Redd. May 09, 2019. Accessed 14 Dec. 2019. https://www.space.com/16758-apollo-11-first-moon-landing.html.

6. "'There's A God Up There': Last Man on the Moon Who Marveled at 'Majestic' Earth Passes into Eternity." Hazel Torres. Fri 20 Jan 2017 16:02 GMT. Accessed 16 Dec. 2019. https://www.christiantoday.com/article/theres-a-god-up-there-last-man-on-the-moon-who-marvelled-at-majestic-earth-passes-into-eternity/104018.htm

7   Franklin, Bill. "The Pearly Moon's No Stopping Place for Me". Oct. 1957. Used by permission.

8   "Rainbow," "God's Bow," (see Genesis 9:12–17). "Colors of the Rainbow in Order." Juan Ramos. October 23, 2017. Accessed 28 Dec. 2019. https://sciencetrends.com/7-colors-rainbow-order/

9   Cerullo, Morris. *Morris Cerullo's Blog: To Know God.*, June 9, 2018. Accessed 14 Dec. 2019. https://morriscerullo.com/to-know-god.

10 Kennett, Jackson B. *The Rainbow and Noah's Ark*. 2017. Used by permission.

CHAPTER II:
HEAVEN: GOD'S ABODE, MAN'S DESITINY

11 *Yoke,* Greek definition: pair of balances (see Matthew 11:29), *Strong's Concordance, Blue Letter Bible*. Accessed 14 Dec. 2019

12 "I Never Said It Would Be Easy." Artist unknown to this author.

13 Kennett, Ronnie S. "The Circle of God's Love." 1978.

14 Lincoln quotation, see online "Abraham Lincoln brainy quotes." Accessed 14 Dec. 2019. https://www.brainyquote.com/quotes/abraham_lincoln_121271

15 *ous*, Greek for "ear," *Strong's Concordance* – metaphor definition – "faculty of understanding and knowing," *Blue Letter Bible*. Accessed 14 Dec. 2019.

16 *Many*, definition: "variety and diversity," from *Merriam-Webster's Collegiate Dictionary*, Eleventh Edition (2007).

CHAPTER III:
NAMES OF THE CITY OF GOD

17 *New, kainos*, NAS *New Testament Greek Lexicon, Blue Letter Bible*. Accessed 14 Dec. 2019. https://www.blueletterbible.org/lang/lexicon/lexicon.cfm?strongs=G2537.

18 Moore, James C. *Never Grow Old*. 1914. Public domain. Accessed 14 Dec. 2019. https://hymnary.org/text/i_have_heard_of_a_land_on_the_far_away_s.

19 *Heavenly music*, Revelation 5:9 (they sang a NEW song); 14:2–3 (the 144 thousand sand a NEW song that no one else can sing); 15:2–3 (those who overcome the antichrist during the great tribulation sing the song of Moses (see Exodus 15:1–21); notice that Exodus 15:11 is the glorious verse quoted in Revelation 15:3); and 19:1, 3, 4, and 6, which is the four Hallelujahs. I believe these four Hallelujahs will be sung, since the Hebrew definition is "Praise Ye the Lord."

20 Kennett, Ronnie S. "Step Up to Meet Jesus." 1986.

21 "Prophecy," definition; Strong's Concordance, Bible Hub, translation is "foretelling and/or forthtelling." Accessed 14 Dec. 2019. https://biblehub.com/greek/4394.htm.

22 Walking with the King, "I Am That I Am," 1983 October, November, December Radio, Family Chat newsletter article titled: "Walking with the King" by Doug Joines, which also contained "Jesus is..." statements set forth in this section of the book.

23 Smith, Pat Marvenko. "The Burning Bush." Used by permission.

24 "Jesus said it...," quoted by several over the years; see 1950 U.S. Senate Committee as stated in online dictionary *Christianese*.

25 *The Majestic Throne of God*, painting by Rita Bennett: "To Ronnie Kennett; Several of the seven pictures from Heaven Tours"; courtesy to use from: Rita M. Bennett, author, copyright 2009, president, Christian Renewal Association, P. O. Box 576, Edmonds, WA 98020 USA"; see, also, www.EmotionallyFree.org.

26 Kennett, Ronnie S. "The Old Old Story." 2001.

CHAPTER IV:
EARTLY COMPARISONS WITH NEW JERUSALEM

27 Smith, Pat Marvenko. "New Jerusalem." Used by permission.

28 Earthly Jerusalem temples (two have been built and one is to be built), "Second Temple," which details Solomon's Temple, Herod's Temple, and a Third Temple (also known as Ezekiel's Temple), yet to be built as many believe, during the tribulation period. Accessed 14 Dec. 2019. http://www.thesecondtempleofsolomon.com/2019.

SECTION II
NEWNESS: NAMES, SONGS, BODIES

CHAPTER V:
COMPARING EARTHLY JERUSALEM WITH NEW JERUSALEM

29 Earthly Jerusalem, "White Limestone." Accessed 14 Dec. 2019.

30 "The Billion Dollar Poem," Charles Osgood (1981), CBS News.

CHAPTER VI:
NEW JERUSALEM'S SIZE

31 Dr. Wilbur M. Smith, The Biblical Doctrine of Heaven, (Chicago, IL: Moody Press, 1968).

32 "International Space Station," by Elizabeth Howell, February 8, 2018. Accessed 14 Dec. 2019. https://www.space.com/16748-international-space-station.html.

33 "Heaven." Jimmy Swaggart. Accessed 16 Nov. 2019. http://countrygospelandbible.com/?p=61. https://www.youtube.com/watch?v=lNQccBRM5fM.

34 34 Franklin, Bill. "Space Flight." 1957. Used by permission.

35 Grave marker of this author's father Hubert Mayo "Buster" Kennett. This inscription is based on lines in Robert Browning's poem "Andrea Del Sarto": "Ah, but a man's reach should exceed his grasp, Or what's a heaven for?" Accessed 27 Mar. 2020. https://www.poetryfoundation.org/poems/43745/andrea-del-sarto.

36 Moore, Marvin and George Campbell, performed by Jim Reeves. "Four Walls." 1957. Accessed 14 Dec. 2019. https://archive.org/details/78_four-walls_jim-reeves-marvin-moore-george-campbell_gbia0005104a.

37 Kennett, Hubert Mayo (this author's father). "He Conquered Sin." 1974. Recorded and used by permission by Frederick Eugene Kennett. Rusty Goodman's Sound Studio. Madisonville, Kentucky.

CHAPTER VII:
SAN ANTONIO RIVER WALK, MILLION DOLLAR HIGHWAY, AND MAGNIFICENT MILE

38 Map of New Jerusalem, painting by Artist Rita Bennett: "To Ronnie Kennett; Several of the seven pictures from Heaven Tours"; courtesy to use from: Rita M. Bennett, author, copyright 2009, president, Christian Renewal Association, P. O. Box 576, Edmonds, WA 98020 USA"; see, also, www.EmotionallyFree.org.

39 Street of Gold/River Walk, online information Wikipedia, San Antonio, Texas; https.//www.visitsanantonio.com/river-walk.

40 Million Dollar Highway, Durango, Colorado; https//www.tripadvisor.com/attraction ...

41 Magnificent Mile, Chicago, Illinois; https//www.themagnificentmile.com/anonymous.

42 When I Walk Up the Streets of Home. Writer is unknown; this song was taught to the author by his father, Hubert Mayo "Buster" Kennett, who learned it from his father.

SECTION III
EARTHLY AND HEAVENLY PROPHETIC EVENTS

CHAPTER VIII:
THE RAPTURE: "COME UP HITHER"

43 Smith, Pat Marvenko. "The Rapture." Used by permission.

44 Smith, Pat Marvenko. "Emerald Throne Scene." Used by permission.

CHAPTER IX:
THE MARRIAGE SUPPER OF THE LAMB

CHAPTER X:
THE SEVEN-YEAR GREAT TRIBULATION

45 Kennett, Ronnie S. "Man's Walls Are Coming Down." 1990.

CHAPTER XI:
THE SECOND COMING OF JESUS CHRIST AND THE BATTLE OF ARMAGEDDON

46 Smith, Pat Marvenko. "King of Kings and Lord of Lords." Used by permission.

CHAPTER XII:
THE MILLENNIAL KINGDOM OF JESUS CHRIST

47 Kirk, James M. "Our Lord's Return to Earth Again." 1894. Public domain. Accessed 14 Dec. 2019. https://hymnary.org/text/i_am_watching_for_the_coming_of_the_glad.

CHAPTER XIII:
THE GREAT WHITE THRONE JUDGMENT

SECTION IV
THE PEARLY WHITE CITY

CHAPTER XIV:
THE WALL, ITS FOUNDATIONS, AND ITS GATES OF PEARL

48 "40 Great Wall of China Facts." Accessed 14 Dec. 2019. https://www.seriousfacts.com/great-wall-of-china-facts.

49 The Tunnel of Light into Heaven, painting by Artist Rita Bennett: "To Ronnie Kennett; Several of the seven pictures from Heaven Tours"; courtesy to use from: Rita M. Bennett, author, copyright 2009, president, Christian Renewal Association, P. O. Box 576, Edmonds, WA 98020 USA"; see, also, www.EmotionallyFree.org.

50 "Nacre" and "iridescence." Accessed 14 Dec. 2019. https://www.wisegeek.com/what-is-nacre.htm.

51 Warren, B. E. Music by C. W. Naylor. "Sin Can Never Enter There." Copyright 1902 by B. E. Warren and owned by R. E. Winsett. Copyright by Tennessee Music & Printing Company in 1951. Accessed 14 Dec. 2019. https://hymnary.org/text/heaven_is_a_holy_place.

52   Smith, Pat Marvenko. "Foundations of the City." Used by permission.

CHAPTER XV:
THE TWELVE PRECIOUS GEMSTONES

53   Kennett, Ronnie S. "Heaven By and By." 1970.

54   WorkWithColor.com. "Colors of the Rainbow." Accessed August 22, 2019. http://www.workwithcolor.com/colors-of-the-rainbow-6987.htm.

55   Morris Cerullo's Blog, "To Know God," by Morris Cerullo, June 9, 2018. Accessed 14 Dec. 2019. https://morriscerullo.com/to-know-god.

56   "Chlorophyll – Biology," Encyclopaedia Brittanica, written by The Editors of Encyclopaedia Brittanica. Accessed 14 Dec. 2019. https://www.britannica.com/science/chlorophyll.

57   Skin-pigmentation defined, Merriam Webster Dictionary; https://www.merriam-webster.com/dictionary/pigmentation

58   Black definition(s), Merriam-Webster Dictionary and Dictionary, Inc. Accessed 14 Dec. 2019. https://www.merriam-webster.com/dictionary/black.

CHAPTER XVI:
HIGH PRIEST BREASTPLATE/PRECIOUS GEMSTONES (OLD TESTAMENT) COMPARED TO NEW JERUSALEM'S PRECIOUS GEMSTONES

59   Bridgewater, A. S. (Mrs.). Music by A. P. Bland. Recitation by George Younce. "How Beautiful Heaven Must Be." Accessed 14 Dec. 2019. http://www.pdhymns.com/SheetMusic/B_Normal/A-H_Normal/H_Normal/How%20Beautiful%20Heaven%20Must%20Be_N.pdf

CHAPTER XVII:
THE PRECIOUS GEMSTONE JASPER

60 Jasper defined. The Merriam-Webster New International Dictionary. Page 1330. Second Edition, Unabridged. Copyright 1959. G & C Merriam Company.

61 Hoffman, Elisha A. "Are You Washed In the Blood." Public Domain. Accessed 14 Dec. 2019. http://www.hymnsuntogod.org/Hymns-PD/A-Hymns/Are-You-Washed-In-The-Blood.html.

CHAPTER XVIII:
THE SOUNDS OF HEAVENLY MUSIC

62 "I'll Be Singing Up There," taken from an African American song. Public Domain.

63 Woolston, C. Herbert. Music by George F. Root. Jesus Loves the Little Children. Accessed 14 Dec. 2019. http://sweetslyrics.com/86284.American%20Songs%20-%20Jesus%20Loves%20the%20Little%20Children.html. Public domain. http://www.pdhymns.com/SheetMusic/Normal/I-Q/J/Jesus%20Loves%20The%20Little%20Children_N.pdf.

64 Roe v. Wade, 410 U.S. 113, 93 S. Ct. 705, 35 L. Ed. 2d 147, 1973 U.S. LEXIS 159 (U.S. Jan. 22, 1973).

65 "Angel" definition, William Smith. Smith's Bible Dictionary, quoted in Blue Letter Bible (1884). Accessed 14 Dec. 2019. https://www.biblestudytools.com/dictionaries/smiths-bible=dictionary/angels.html

SECTION V
ETTERNITY WITH GOD AND THE LAMB

CHAPTER XIX:
SIGHTS AND SOUNDS OF THE TREE OF LIFE

66. "H8104 - shamar - Strong's Hebrew Lexicon (KJV)." Blue Letter Bible. Accessed 16 Nov. 2019. https://www.blueletterbible.org//lang/lexicon/lexicon.cfm?Strongs=H8104&t=KJV.

67. "H1870 - derek - Strong's Hebrew Lexicon (KJV)." Blue Letter Bible. Accessed 16 Nov. 2019. https://www.blueletterbible.org//lang/lexicon/lexicon.cfm?Strongs=H1870&t=KJV.

68. Pannell, Joe. Let Me Rest. 1929. Accessed 14 Dec. 2019. https://hymnary.org/text/theres_a_fountain_thats_free.

69. Salem Kirban Reference Bible (1979), copyright #79-53475, page 354.

70. Salem Kirban Reference Bible (1979), copyright #79-53475, page 354.

CHAPTER XX:
SIGHTS AND SOUNDS OF THE RIVER OF LIFE

71. Springer, Rebecca Ruter. My Dream of Heaven, Intra Muros. First publication 1898, republished by Vicki Jamison-Peterson Ministries, Harrison House Publishers, 2002.

72. Albert Brumley-Stamps/Baxter. I'll Meet You by the River. 1942. Accessed 14 Dec. 2019. https://hymnary.org/text/over_on_the_bright_elysian_shore.

CHAPTER XXI:
NO MORE CURSE

73. Parker, Rex and Eleanor Parker. The Curse Shall Be Lifted Some Day. 1950s.

74 Ingler, Arthur F. "The Pearly White City." Copyright 1929. Renewed by Nazarene Pub. House, Owner. Public Domain Accessed 28 Dec. 2019. http://www.pdhymns.com/SheetMusic/Normal/R-Z/T/The%20Pearly%20White%20City_N.pdf.

75 Crosby, Fanny J. Music by George C. Stebbins Saved by Grace. Words, Copyright 1891. Music, Copyright 1894. Public Domain. Accessed: 28 Dec. 2019. http://www.hymnpod.com/2010/04/11/saved-by-grace.

CHAPTER XXII:
NO MORE NIGHT AND SUPER SUNDAY

76 Vernon McGee, TH.D.L.L.D., "Thru the Bible." Ordained Presbyterian minister. Accessed 14 Nov, 2019. https://ttb.org.

77 Jenson, Gordon. "Jesus Will Outshine Them All." Copyright 1972. John T. Benson Pub. Co. Accessed: 28 Dec. 2019. https://www.pine-net.com/babcockstore/outshine.htm. Recorded and used by permission by Frederick Eugene Kennett. Artist Recording Co. Cincinnati, Ohio.

78 Kennett, Ronnie S. Super Sunday. 1983.

CHAPTER XXIII:
REIGNING FOREVER WITH GOD THE FATHER, JESUS CHRIST THE SON, AND THE HOLY SPIRIT

79 "G4821 - symbasileuō - Strong's Greek Lexicon (KJV)." Blue Letter Bible. Accessed 16 Nov, 2019. https://www.blueletterbible.org//lang/lexicon/lexicon.cfm?Strongs=G4821&t=KJV

80 President Eisenhower's One Nation Under God. Accessed 17 Oct. 2019. https://wallbuilders.com/president-eisenhowers-one-ntion-god/.

81 Ingler, Arthur F. "The Pearly White City." Copyright 1929. Renewed by Nazarene Pub. House, Owner. Public Domain. Accessed 28 Dec. 2019. http://www.pdhymns.com/SheetMusic/Normal/R-Z/T/The%20Pearly%20White%20City_N.pdf.

82 "Jesus, Welcome Home." Artist unknown to this author.

CPSIA information can be obtained
at www.ICGtesting.com
Printed in the USA
BVHW021452290620
582433BV00006B/14